Perfect Phrases for Dealing with Difficult People

Perfect Phrases for Dealing with Difficult People

Hundreds of Ready-to-Use Phrases for Handling Conflict, Confrontations, and Challenging Personalities

Susan F. Benjamin

McGraw-Hill

New York   Chicago   San Francisco   Lisbon
London   Madrid   Mexico City   Milan   New Delhi
San Juan   Seoul   Singapore   Sydney   Toronto

8 9 0   QFR/QFR   0

ISBN–13: 978–0–07–149304–8
ISBN–10: 0–07–149304–2

McGraw-Hill books are available at special quantity discounts to use as premiums and sales promotions, or for use in corporate training programs. For more information, please write to the Director of Special Sales, Professional Publishing, McGraw-Hill, Two Penn Plaza, New York, NY 10121–2298. Or contact your local bookstore.

This book is printed on acid-free paper.

To Mary Roadruck, whose outrageous humor and goodwill are the perfect anecdotes for difficult people everywhere.

Contents

Acknowledgments xi

Part One: What You Need to Know

Why Address Difficult People   3
Top Seven Imperatives of Communicating with
    Difficult People   4

**Part Two: Perfect Phrases for Communicating
with Difficult Coworkers**

Unfriendly Coworkers   15
Coworkers Who Withhold   17
Petty and Gossipy Coworkers   21
Argumentative People   26
Loud and Obnoxious Coworkers   32
Negative Coworkers   36
When That Negative, Angry, or Difficult Employee Is You   41

**Part Three: Perfect Phrases for
Communicating with Difficult Bosses**

Bully Bosses   47
Unfocused and Forgetful Bosses   52

Contents

Distant, Weak, or Hands-Off Bosses   57

How to Ask for an Overdo Promotion or Raise   62

Micromanagers   66

How to Correct Your Boss's Mistakes   71

How to Get a Letter of Recommendation from a
   Reluctant Boss   74

How to Say Good-bye to a Problem Boss—Without
   Burning Bridges   78

Part Four: Perfect Phrases for Communicating with Difficult Employees

Complainers   85

How to Address Inappropriate Behavior, Dress,
   or Hygiene   90

Employees Who Spread Rumors   96

Lazy or Lethargic Employees   99

Passive-Aggressive Employees   107

Angry Employees   115

Stuck-in-the-Box Performers   124

How to Settle Disputes Between Employees   131

How to Motivate Employees Who Resist Change   138

Part Five: Perfect Phrases for Communicating with Difficult Customers

Angry Customers   151

Antsy and Anxious Customers   159

How to Help Customers Adapt to Changes   163

How to Resolve Billing Problems with Customers   169

How to Manage Demanding Customers   177

Contents

Part Six: Perfect Phrases for Communicating with Difficult Vendors and Employees from Other Departments

How to Control a Coworker from Another Department in a
    Meeting with Customers   187
Difficult Contractors   193
Difficult Vendors and Suppliers   199
How to Negotiate Finances with Difficult Vendors
    and Contractors   206
Disruptive Participants in Presentations   210

Acknowledgments

I'd like to start by acknowledging all those *not* difficult people who have helped me with this project: most notably my agent, Grace Freedson, who's more than easy to talk to—she's fun. Thanks also to my editor at McGraw Hill, Donya Dickerson, and all those other helpful folks I've encountered throughout this project.

Also, thanks to Janice Seimsen and Sandy Rawdon for their interest in a related project, as well as to those folks who make sure my books get into the laps of readers: Mary Roadruck, Michael Dresser, Susan Greenman, and those wonderful publicity people I've met over the years. Of course, big thanks go to my son, Adam. Trying to teach him how to deal with difficult people, and not become one himself, has been a pretty amazing task.

Last, and most important, a big thanks to all those truly difficult people I have met over the years. You know who you are, and the lessons you taught me have been indispensable!

Part One

What You Need to Know

Why Address Difficult People

Managing Your Expectations—and Theirs

Why confront, e-mail, or otherwise communicate with difficult people at work? People who, say, drive you crazy, cause work slowdowns, and make life miserable every time they can? Many people believe the reasons go something like this: "I want to put my foot down once and for all." Or "I've got to get these feelings off my chest." Or "I'm going to tell that guy what he can do with his attitude." And sometimes there are other, even less savory reasons.

But here's a reality check: The *real* reason to communicate with difficult people is to improve your work life and theirs, not to mention the lives of your boss, coworkers, and, most important, customers. Even when those difficult people *are* the customers. As for whether you like those people or they like you, whether you become bosom buddies or maintain a respectful distance is inconsequential.

Granted, you will need different strategies for communicating with different people. The angry customers must be calmed and controlled while the lethargic employees must be energized. You can use the following tips in all your work interactions, and they will boost your communication to the most successful level possible.

With that in mind, read the following seven imperatives and apply them no matter who is causing you trouble.

Top Seven Imperatives of Communicating with Difficult People

1. Be Objective

Objective language can be your best friend when communicating with difficult people, and it is often the only way to get the response you want. Trust me, it's helpful outside of work also—with difficult neighbors, children, and even friends.

So what is objective language? Say a coworker is disruptive. That's *your* subjective opinion. Will the coworker agree? Doubtful. But if you present objective facts and rely on what you saw and heard, then the true situation becomes clear *and* undeniable. Does your coworker talk too much at meetings? Stop in your office to chat … on an hourly basis … and break your work flow? With those facts at hand, now your coworker can identify the problem exactly.

Look at the difference between subjective and objective language here:

Subjective: You are irritating to other employees who want to get work done.

Objective: You interrupt people by dropping by their work space to chat.

Subjective: You're really annoying in meetings.

Objective: You need to stay in the meetings and talk only when the facilitator calls on you.

Subjective: You don't respect other people.

Objective: You routinely call other people derogatory names.

Even better, once the person can understand the problem objectively, he or she can find the solution. Call other people names? Well, stop doing it.

2. Use Examples

When discussing a person's bad behavior at work, the response you get may be "Huh?" as in "I have *no* idea what you're talking about," even though you've been objective and clear, and—face it—it's such an obvious problem *everyone* knows what you're talking about, even the cleaning staff. So use an example to illustrate what you mean. Let's get back to an example from the last section on objective language—"You need to stay in the meetings and talk only when the facilitator calls on you."

Assuming your coworker doesn't have a bladder problem, that's a fair request. Yet your coworker responds with an open mouth and hurt expression as if to say, "But I *do* sit in the meetings. I never miss a *word*." Your only recourse is to provide an example, such as "Yesterday, at the managers' meeting, you got up three times." Then, lest the coworker claim the event was a mere exception to otherwise great meeting etiquette, give another example: "And during my presentation last week, you were in and out at least two times."

If, rather than your coworker, this person happens to be your employee, record these examples. Be clear about names, dates, and other specifics. You may need them later.

3. Commit to the Accuracy Principle

Be accurate. Always. Say, for example, you accused that annoying coworker of walking out on meetings "about 10 times." Granted, you didn't literally mean 10 times—you were only trying to make a point. But, sadly, the point was lost in the exaggeration of the number. Are you a manager? Then accuracy is a must in your performance reviews too—especially with difficult employees. Being accurate can foster trust, motivate employees to change their behavior, and enhance the goodwill about everything from potential pay increases to awards.

Regardless of whether you're dashing off a quick e-mail or writing a formal written review, use exact, supportable, and, yes, objective language by addressing these questions:

- What was the degree of the behavior? How did you determine that?
- How often did it occur?
- What were the direct repercussions? How can you measure them?
- Did you or anyone else confront this problem before? When and how often?

4. Take Advantage of Venues

All forms of messages are not equal. People retain considerably more of the written word than the spoken word, provided that they actually read it. Still, in face-to-face discussions, you can get cues to help you refine or otherwise position your message, whether a quizzical expression, a smile, or a subtle shake of the head.

Here are a few pointers that can help.

Written Message

- The first few words are critical: They're the ones people remember and will set a tone for the rest.

■ Avoid unnecessarily formal language. It can sound unduly angry, cold, or alienating. Granted, you don't want to use syrupy phrases either. But keep the tone neutral or, if you dare, friendly.

■ Have lots of points? Are you addressing a rebel employee who refuses to follow procedures? Use bullets, numbers, or steps. They're easy to see and impossible *not* to follow.

Spoken Message

■ Employees and coworkers hear only every fifth word or so, and that means you need to repeat key points throughout the discussion.

■ Watch for body language—yours and your employee's or coworker's. Sit down to talk and see that your employee or coworker has crossed arms and an indirect gaze? This could signal hostility. But continue watching his or her body language throughout the discussion for signs that you're being effective. Watch your own body language too. Are you expressing fear or anger? Or openness about finding a solution and moving on?

Don't forget to take control of the environment around you. Want to give the impression of power? Then sit at the head of the table. Want to appear relaxed and conciliatory? Then sit at a seat across the table. Also, choose *where* you're meeting carefully. Meeting in a conference room? That's usually neutral space. A café signals a friendly space. An office? The power belongs to the person whose office you're in.

5. Follow Your Vision

There's no question that difficult people are a pain to be around—especially coworkers whom you see day after day after day. They create hostility, uneasiness, and problems. Half the time, they *are* the problem. And you may not like them. But in the end, all that matters is how they affect your work and your unit's work. So when taking a difficult person to task, conjure a vision of how the perfect situation would look. That vision could be small scale, like that guy who's always interrupting meetings. Your vision: to sit through meetings from beginning to end without interruptions. Or the vision could be large scale: for your unit to meet all of its financial goals, get great bonuses and extra paid time off, and have a friendly, energetic work environment … then, when you're communicating with the difficult person, connect his or her behavior to that vision. This will turn a complaint into a serious work issue. Here are some examples:

Complaint: You're not a team player, which hurts every one of us.

Vision oriented: We want to increase sales by more than 75 percent this quarter. But since you've been late with the quotes four out of five times, we probably won't get close.

Complaint : You don't seem to realize that this isn't a social club. We just can't spend time hanging out and talking all day.

Vision oriented: If we're going to meet all our deadlines, as we discussed in October's meeting, we must limit our socializing to lunch breaks.

6. Keep Records

If you're a manager, you have one critical record stored away: the performance review. Make the most of this record. Don't be shy about discussing problems and concrete ways your employees can overcome them. If your problem is with a coworker, customer, or boss, you should still keep records of your interactions—you may need them later. Record events, plus the days and times they occurred. Have any witnesses? Write their names down too. Also, be sure to save

- E-mails and other messages from fellow employees.
- Notes about when the employee exhibited negative behavior.
- Notes about conversations you had with the employee.
- Follow-up e-mails to the employee about agreements you made in one-on-one discussions.
- Project management documents indicating how the employee affected work flow.

7. When in Doubt

Have questions? Do you find that difficult employee overwhelming or even frightening? Don't make the two *biggest* mistakes possible: using guesswork and avoiding the situation. Instead, talk to your manager or call your HR department. No question, they can help.

Part Two

Perfect Phrases for Communicating with Difficult Coworkers

Communicating with coworkers can be strange. They're not exactly friends, although you do chat in the halls and know, for example, about their crazy kids and unfortunate divorces. They're not business partners, subordinates, or managers. And certainly, as much as you crave it, you can't tell them where to put their attitude on a bad day. So communicating with them is bound to be … interesting. Challenging. And problematic.

Naturally you'd think somewhere along the line someone in a business class, graduate school, or even a creative writing course would have tipped you off about how to communicate with difficult coworkers. But no—you're thrust in the workplace with coworkers who drive you crazy, and there seems to be no right way to tell them to stop.

What's an employee to do? Here are three pointers:

1. *Keep it professional:* Coworkers keeping critical data to themselves? It could be that they want control of the project. Granted, that stinks, but it isn't about *you* personally. That means your response *isn't* to say you find them contemptible—a personal and unwise choice—but to emphasize the reason you are professionally entitled to the data.

2. *Document as if your professional life depended on it—which, by the way, it might:* That means write every agreement you make with your coworkers, even over coffee in the office kitchenette, and e-mail it to them. Then save a copy for yourself. Oh, and record everything else of consequence, even small consequence, and save that too. You never know when the notes of today will become career-saving content of tomorrow.

3. *Use strategy:* Communication is never just what you say, write, or project with body language. It contains layers and layers of innuendos, so you need to strategize. Sure, the words that rush to your mouth may be to tell your coworkers what maniacs they are—but don't do it. Decide what you want professionally; then strategize how to say it right. And what should drive that decision? The response that will ultimately help you, and your team, at work.

Not sure what to say? You did the right thing by turning to this part of the book. You'll find lots of perfect phrases for just about every brand of difficult coworkers, from gossips to chronic arguers, and some quick tips that will also help.

Unfriendly Coworkers

Your objective with unfriendly employees isn't to become bosom buddies, although that's always nice. Instead, you need to create a synergy so that you can work together—as professionals. Think your coworkers don't like you for a personal reason? The way you laugh? Your hairstyle? Or is it that you're outgoing and they're not? Be courteous and move on. But if you think you've offended your coworkers for some reason, find out why. Remember, make the discussion as objective as possible.

Statements to Avoid

- You're really being rude to me.
- I really hate how you're treating me.
- I used to think you were okay, but now I just think you're nasty.
- Do you dislike me for some reason? If so, you should tell me what it is.
- Do you have a problem with me?
- What's going on with you? You're like a cold fish these days, and it kind of stinks.

Statements to Use

When Coworkers Suddenly Get Cold

- I hope I haven't done anything to offend you.
- Would you like to discuss any issues with me?
- Did something happen that I don't know about?
- Have I said something you think is inappropriate?
- Is there anything I've done to obstruct this project? If so, I'd like to know what it is.

When Coworkers Are Rude or Unpleasant

- If you have an issue with me, let me know. Otherwise, I expect that you'll treat me with respect.
- I don't respond to that kind of language. Let me know when you're ready to talk.
- I think we need to discuss this project, but only in civil terms.
- If you want me to engage in this discussion, you must treat me respectfully.
- I assume you have something useful to say, but it's impossible for me to hear when you speak that way.
- We need to talk in a professional manner.

Quick tip: Think a coworker is abusive? Then document your interactions and write down anyone who witnessed them. And contact your HR department immediately.

Coworkers Who Withhold

Coworkers may withhold information for a variety of reasons. Perhaps they're too busy. Or maybe they don't know the processes and procedures for passing it on. Or perhaps they're forgetful. Worse, they may be trying to get in the way of your professional advancement because they're jealous or want that position for themselves. No matter, you need to maintain as professional and objective a stance in getting that information from them—not once, but on an ongoing basis. Here's how.

Connect Your Request with a Professional Outcome

- Please send me the financial records for FY 06 so I can complete the audit.
- I need to have updates so that I can revise the policy procedure.
- Let me know about the pricing changes so that we can give the customer accurate information.
- Please forward the project plan so that I can assign the right people to each role and responsibility.
- We must have the missing data if we are to complete the project.
- If you don't send the meeting notes by 6:00, I cannot complete the presentation.

Show How Your Team Is Affected By the Situation

The if-then structure works well here:

- If we are to get the full budget, then you must send us …
- If we are to make our deadline, then be sure to supply …
- If our team is to work cohesively, then you must keep us updated.

Or use the if-then structure in reverse:

- If you provide the updated manual, then we can expedite the process.
- If you get us directions for the new tool, then we can communicate faster.
- If you tell us the plans in advance, then we can prepare the right documentation.

Use Specific Sentence Structures

Have a long, dreary history with withholding coworkers? Does everyone suffer as a result? Then it's helpful to use a sentence structure that goes something like this:

Action   Outcome   Solution

Here are a few examples:

- (*action*) Since you omitted two pages on last year, (*outcome*) we didn't get the grant, (*solution*) so this time, please provide everything we need.
- (*action*) Because you didn't get us the complete financials, (*outcome*) we missed the deadline last year. (*solution*) So please send all six statements by Friday.

You Can Mix Up the Order Too

Take a look at these examples:

- Our customers had to wait in long lines last week because you didn't notify us that you were assigned to the other branch. Please let us know about changes immediately so that we can fill your slot.

- We have been late on four of the five reports because you didn't get us your section until after the deadline. Please send everything we need by the fifteenth so that we won't continue to repeat the situation.

Be Specific about When You Requested the Information Before

- As I mentioned in the meeting on Friday, …
- Twice last week, on Tuesday and Friday, I left you voice mails about sending the …
- As you probably recall from our discussion at the staff meeting, you need to supply …
- Tony and I contacted you three times last week for the …
- As I requested in my e-mails on February 10, 12, and 15, we need to receive …
- In the meeting on Monday and the follow-up on Tuesday, you agreed to provide …
- Even though I e-mailed you reminders every day since, you still haven't complied.

Refer to a Source

Give a policy or procedure that says the coworker must send you the information:

- As our communications flowchart clearly indicates, …
- On page 62 of our Policies and Procedures Manual, it states that you must inform us of …
- In the meeting, our boss said that you should get us the …

- If you look on the project plan, you'll see that your role is to keep us informed of ...
- Since all the data flow through your office, the organizational chart show that you are responsible for ...

> *Quick tip:* Remember to e-mail your requests for information even if you had a conversation about the requests first. That way, should the slowdowns from withholding coworkers create project break-downs, you'll be protected.

Petty and Gossipy Coworkers

Pettiness and gossip usually run rampant in the workplace. And why? On the positive side (and *yes* there is a positive side!), they inform employees about what to expect from each other. This creates a sense of predictability and makes projects easier to control. On the negative side, well, you've probably been on the receiving end more than once. Pettiness and gossip can be wildly disproportionate, packed with lies, and mean-spirited. For your own sake and the sake of your workplace, you need to deal with it.

The best way is to redirect the conversation so it has a more work-related orientation. Look at the difference between the two:

Petty: She loves hoarding information. It's her way to make herself feel powerful because she's really insecure and mean.

Work related: She usually takes days, even longer, to respond no matter how many e-mails you send.

Petty: I think he's crazy. I wouldn't trust him for anything in the world.

Work related: The logic in the reports often doesn't come together, and he frequently gets facts wrong.

The following section provides other perfect phrases that can help.

In One-to-One Discussions

An Employee Makes a Personal Assault on Another Employee Under the Guise of Being Businesslike

- How do these issues affect the assignment?
- That personal issue aside, what are her responsibilities?
- Actually, I'm not concerned about her personal issues but her input into the project.
- Let's focus on her contributions to the project and how we can succeed.
- So what is the best approach for working with him?

In this situation, it can be helpful to put the onus on the employee making the comment:

- So how do you intend to work with him to get the best results?
- What are some ways you can approach her for the best response?
- What steps do you plan to take so that you can work together?

An Employee Calls Another Employee Names

Make no mistake, name-calling is damaging, abusive, and wrong. Here are some ways, albeit blunt, to stop those remarks:

- Let's not act like kids, calling names. Just tell me how her work style will affect the project.
- I'd rather not hear that kind of comment.
- Saying things like that isn't remotely useful. What do I need to know about his role in this project?
- What does that mean in terms of my working with her?

One Employee Quotes Another's Disparaging Remarks

- Bill shouldn't make comments like that, and we shouldn't repeat them.
- Let's focus on more productive ways of discussing work.
- That's her opinion, but it isn't helpful.
- I'm not interested in those kinds of comments.
- Next time, just tell Elizabeth to avoid those kinds of remarks.

An Employee Relies on Rumor to Assert His or Her Position

In this situation, *first* squelch the rumor and then readjust the conversation so that you can move ahead. Here's how:

- We don't have any evidence that this is the case, so let's look at what we know.
- I haven't heard anything like that. Let's steer clear of rumor. Now what do we have that's documented?
- I don't know how that rumor surfaced, but let's squelch it immediately. Here's what I do know, though.
- Let's stick to the facts now. If anything changes, I'll let you know.

> *Quick tip:* Often it's best to ignore the petty or gossipy remark altogether. Eventually, the gossipy employee will take the hint. In other situations, though, you will need to respond quickly and effectively.

In Meetings

One Employee Alludes to Another's Personality in a Negative and Disparaging Way

- It's important that we stay focused on the subject at hand and avoid personal feelings.
- We must act in the most professional manner possible.
- We are all colleagues on an important mission. My expectation is that we will treat other people as such in this meeting and everywhere else.
- Our goal is to solve our unit's problems—not discuss personality issues.
- I don't want to discuss personality traits. We need to focus on accomplishing our goals.

An Employee Makes Faces or Negative Sounds Even When the Object of the Insults Is in the Room

Make your point to the group in general to avoid an embarrassing situation for everyone:

- I've noticed that several people are acting unprofessionally. Please stop.
- We can't continue this meeting until everyone here approaches the discussion in the most professional way possible.
- My expectation is that we will work as a team—which means everyone must be respectful and professional.
- I think we all need to approach each other as professionals and equals in this meeting, and elsewhere.

In E-Mails

You Want to Address Specific Remarks That Occurred in a Meeting

- At the last meeting, several people made personal remarks that caused others to feel uncomfortable. Please refrain from such comments in the November 5 meeting—and in the office in general.
- You are among the most professional workers in our field. Please exercise that professionalism in our meetings and avoid making disparaging remarks.
- Remember, we are guided by policies that require professional behavior in word and action.
- Focus all your comments in the most productive and objective way possible—in meetings and in the office.

Argumentative People

One thing about argumentative coworkers is that they love to argue—and not necessarily because they believe in their point. No, the reasons argumentative people argue are typically personal and rooted in deep personal problems. Maybe they have a mental illness or a personality disorder, or they fall under the vague header of "impossible." No matter, when dealing with argumentative people, you can't win. So don't even bother trying—just avoid engaging or confronting them. But when work requires that you interact, take this three-part approach.

Step 1. Get Control of the Discussion Before It Starts

Focus On the Outcome of Your Communication So That You Can Maintain a Clear Direction and Sense of Purpose

- We need to decide dates and places for …
- We have to decide which of the technology tools we're going to use.
- Can you tell me which of the candidates you like best?
- If you want to change any of these steps, just indicate how.

> *Quick tip:* Do *not* ask argumentative people for their opinions because doing that is a clear invitation for controversy. Instead, describe *specifically* what you need.

Create Clear Parameters for Your Discussion
Numbers or dates can help here so that you can establish an end to the communication:

➡

- Let us know which one of the four candidates you like best.
- What are the two best ways we can proceed with this project?
- Give me two times when you are available for the meeting.
- Please let us know your thoughts on the project by the fourteenth—at the latest.
- If you have problems or want to make changes, e-mail me your ideas by 5:00 on Friday.
- If you want to change or add anything to this proposal, let me know by 3:00 on Tuesday. The deadline is 5:00.

Base the Course of Your Communication on a Policy or Other Organizational Agreement

- Make any changes by the sixteenth because the regulation requires we respond by then.
- The manual says you need to give your input in two paragraphs or less.
- According to our contract, you can make changes to Steps 3 and 4 but not 1 or 2.
- I agree that you are an expert on this subject, but the job description indicates that this is Joel's area of responsibility.
- Even though I'd like to get your comments on all aspects of this study, the project plan indicates that you are responsible for page 1.
- If you look at the flowchart, you'll see that you're responsible for this assignment, although I'm sure you'd contribute a great deal to the others.

Use a Good-Behavior Reward Strategy, but Be Discreet

- If you limit your changes to three or four lines, we can get this proposal in on time.
- Please check with me before organizing the workshops so that I can maximize the number of people who attend.
- We're asking everyone to save his or her opinions for after the meeting so that we can be out by 5:00.
- If this meeting goes smoothly and everyone works well together, we can put you on the team.
- If we can move through this process quickly, we'll reach our unit's goals. And that means bonuses for all of us.

Step 2. Move the Discussion in a Productive Direction If It Gets Derailed

Since argumentative people have a passion for power, they may quickly derail the discussion. Your job requires ultimate self-control. That means, *don't* try to win, *don't* take the bait no matter how tempting it is, and *don't* get caught up in the argument. And remember, argumentative people *love* to find your weak spots. Make it clear that you want to avoid conflict, and conflict is what you'll get. So avoid disclaimers like these, which will only fuel your argumentative coworkers.

Phrases to Avoid
- I don't want to argue with you.
- Let's discuss this peacefully.
- I'm sure we can come to agreement quickly if …

Instead, stick to the specific outcomes we reviewed a minute ago.

Should the Discussion Become Volatile, Use "Understanding" Words to Diffuse It

- I understand what you mean.
- That's an interesting point.
- Yes, I know many people feel that way.
- Okay, I see your point.
- I see what you're saying.

Then move on in the conversation, quickly shifting gears. Be sure to use neutral connecting terms.

Avoid Using These

- But
- Actually
- Not really
- Unfortunately
- But the truth is

Instead, Use These

- Next
- Also
- Now

Some Examples

- I understand what you're saying. Next we need to discuss …
- Yes, that's an insightful perspective. We also need to review …
- Thanks for letting me know your opinion. Now we need to decide …

> *Quick tip:* Argumentative people need to feel important—in power and in control. So avoid using negating words that might offend them, albeit subtly. You won't be changing your point, and you will be stifling a potential fire.

Negating Words to Avoid

Only

- We want you to change only paragraphs 3 and 4.
- You can come only to the meeting for entry-level managers.
- We need experts only in technology—not in your field.

Just

- You just have to tell us the name, not all the details.
- The boss wants you to participate in just this part of the project.
- You are just an advisor on this project.

Step 3. Reinforce, Restate, or Repeat Your Conclusion

- So the next step will be for us …
- These are the changes you want.
- What you agreed to do is …
- Your opinion is that …
- Your three responsibilities will be to …
- Of the four choices, you like the first and second the best.

Incorporate Your Employees' Conclusions

Give them ownership of the outcome later—they're less likely to disagree with their own decisions:

- As you suggested, we used the technology tool from Delta-Plus.
- We liked your idea about leaving that information out of the proposal, so we kept it out.
- Your idea of putting Joan in customer service was good, and we used it.
- We appreciated your feedback, and we decided to use your ideas on … [*Discuss the ideas you did use and not the ones you didn't use.*]
- This is the approach that you suggested in the meeting last Tuesday.

Loud and Obnoxious Coworkers

We all know these types of coworkers. How could we not? They make themselves known. On the up side, some are jokesters, quick with a guffaw, a "good morning," and an amusing, albeit often off-color, joke. On the down side, they draw negative attention to themselves and derail discussions. Of course, some obnoxious employees are worse than others. Think a coworker is insulting or otherwise harassing you at work? Notify your manager or call HR. For situations that do not need to be referred to HR, here are some great things to do.

> *Quick tip:* Use humor, but remember the difference between a confrontational comment and a funny one can depend on your tone. So keep it light.

Use Humor

- Oh, there goes Harold again.
- Thanks for the input Harold [*said ironically and comically*].
- Another country heard from.
- And, moving right along, …
- Uh-huh, sure. And thank you, Harold. Anyone else?
- Great. Thanks much, Harold.

Rein In the Conversation

- Anyway, as we were saying, …
- Let's hear from someone else now. Jennifer, do you have anything to add?

- Okay, but we still need to determine where we're going from here.
- Let's get back to the point, which is …
- What I really want to know, though, is …
- Humm. Did we ever finish discussing where we're going to …
- We really need to stay on target here and take this project seriously or we'll never complete it.

Remind Them of the Circumstances Around Them

- Let's talk softer so we don't disturb the meeting down the hall.
- We need to be quiet in this area, since people are working.
- A lot of customers are around—we need to keep this really professional.
- The boss talked to several people about noise control last week, so let's keep it down, okay?
- We have to be really professional when we're in this department.
- Better be careful. The chief is around, and we need to make a good impression.
- Don't talk too loudly here. Sound is really amplified.

Quick tip: With loud coworkers, rely on voice control. Just lower your voice, and your coworkers will naturally lower theirs too. If that doesn't work, use hand gestures, like lowering your palms in the air, to signal to them that they're being too loud.

Let Your Coworkers Know That You Have Their Well-Being and Interests in Mind

- You're such a great person and offer so much to this unit. I'd hate to see you limit your potential with comments like that.
- I want to tell you something because I like you and want to see you succeed.
- Do you mind if I make a personal comment that I hope will help you?
- Everyone here really seems to like you, and you are a great guy, but you get in your own way when you make off-color jokes like that.
- I know you're just trying to have fun, but when you tease people like that, you sometimes hurt their feelings.
- I know what you mean when you make cracks like that, but I don't think other people do.

> *Quick tip:* Confront your coworkers privately about their behavior and afterward remind them of the discussion as circumstances require.

If Coworkers Make Inappropriate Sexual Comments or Racial Slurs, Take the Following Steps

- I really don't like hearing that kind of thing.
- Please don't say that kind of thing when I'm around.
- Our company has a policy against the use of racially insensitive language.
- When you say things like that, you make me, and everyone else I know, uncomfortable.

Remember, if you don't confront your colleagues' rude or insulting comments—even if they're not targeting you—then you're condoning them.

If Coworkers Embarrass You or Someone Else in the Room

Comment with a Light Tone

- That's really hilarious—but not actually true.
- There he goes again. You never know what he'll say. But let's get back to …
- That's classic, Carolyn. But what's really significant here is …
- Ba-da-bum [*sounds like the drum following a night club comedian's joke*].
- Thanks, Harry. Next?

Refute Them Gently

- Actually, this is how it really is: …
- He always says things like that. The truth is that …
- We need to be as accurate as possible about this. Here's the truth.
- Now be nice, Annie.
- Okay, let's take a different direction here, people.

> *Quick tip:* Don't reprimand or embarrass your coworkers, because that will only embarrass others in the room too. Instead, either comment on what they're saying with a light tone or gently refute their statements. You can discuss the seriousness of their behavior in private later on.

Negative Coworkers

When confronting negative coworkers, you have choices. You can ignore the complaints altogether. Trust me, they'll soon know you aren't an audience for their misery. Or you can respond to what they're saying by showing them the positive side of the situation. For example, if a coworker says this,

> I hate this new system. Why couldn't we just stay with old one? They're always making things difficult.

you can respond with this,

> But it will save us time in the long run.

> Keep your responses realistic. If you're disingenuous, your coworkers will know. Here are a few other tips and perfect phrases for dealing with negative coworkers.

Acknowledge the Validity of What They're Saying

Then move them in a more positive direction:

- I know the new boss is difficult, but she'll really give us the push our unit needs to move ahead.
- Yes, the new hires do chat a lot. But I think we can mentor them so that they become really strong workers.
- It's true. We have been waiting a long time to start the new project. But at least we've had a chance to catch up on some of the other work that's been lagging.
- Yes, everyone agrees with you on that. However, you must admit that …
- That's an interesting point. Only the way I see it is …
- You have mentioned before that you feel this way. But I think we can find several benefits in this situation even though they may not be immediately evident.

➡

Keep Them Focused on the Future

Don't let them get stuck on how bad things currently are:

- If we take these additional steps, who knows what we'll find.
- If we can learn to work with them, we might see improvements.
- In similar situations, though, the results have been really good. For example, …
- Maybe you shouldn't be on that team. Perhaps the boss can move you.
- I think if you approach all customers as potential friends, then …
- Even though we haven't been trained to manage these situations, there are a lot of books on the subject that can help.
- Maybe we should find other ways to reach these goals.

Get Negative People to Find Positive Perspectives Themselves

- What do you think will solve that problem?
- You were involved in a similar situation last quarter. How did your team work it out?
- What happened the last time you used that procedure? It was successful, right?

Give Your Questions Parameters

Spelling out what you're looking for as closely as possible will help them focus on the answers:

- What were the three things that helped when you were in this situation last year?

- How much profit did you need to make to recover last quarter?
- What are the three phrases that have worked with other customers—and that we can use here?

Use "Up" and Future-Oriented Words and Phrases Like These

- Move ahead/forward
- Keep going
- Keep it up
- Shoot high
- Achieve
- Progress
- Accomplish
- Produce

Avoid "Down" Words and Phrases

Look at the difference in these expressions compared with the up-looking ones:

Down- and behind-looking expressions: If we don't pull off this deal, we're in deep trouble.

Up- and ahead-looking expressions: If we get this deal, we'll really be ahead.

Down- and behind-looking expressions: We can't stay behind the other units in sales.

Up- and ahead-looking expressions: We need to exceed the other units in sales.

Now look at these perfect phrases for dealing with negative coworkers.

Coworkers Are Critical of an Important Project

- I understand how you feel, but we really need to move ahead with the project. So what do you think we should do?
- Actually, the boss knows what she's doing, and she must have a good reason for initiating this project.
- We need to decide how we're going to make this project a success, regardless of how you feel about it.
- Moving ahead, how do you think we can make this work?
- I really need to find ways to accomplish what we need with this project. Do you have any ideas?

Coworkers Complain Nonstop

- At this point, I really want to hear what you like.
- I really see things differently. This is what I think: …
- Actually, I think most of these things are pretty good.
- Do you have any solutions to these problems that you're raising?
- In spite of all these problems, I think we've come really far.
- I've heard you mention this before. Maybe you should try a new perspective.
- I see these issues you've been raising in a totally different way.
- Maybe you should start thinking of what you can do to improve the project/workplace/situation.

Coworkers Constantly Respond with Objections or Negativity

- Before you object, hear what I have to say.
- How do you think we can make this project work?
- Please tell me what you like about …
- What about this project do you find interesting?
- How do you think we can make this project better?
- How can we make this idea become a reality?

When That Negative, Angry, or Difficult Employee Is You

Overwhelmed with negative thoughts? When things at work get stressful, unpredictable, or otherwise tough, who isn't? But negativity can hurt your productivity and demoralize everyone around you. While you can't practice mind control, you can apply the principles of self-talk. Every time you hear that negative voice in your head, talk back to it. After a while, you'll change your own thinking and even come to solutions much faster. Here are a few examples:

Negative thought: I get so sick of the deadlines.

Positive self-talk: I have a lot of experience keeping up with deadlines. That's why I'm so good at doing it.

Negative thought: Why must our priority list change so much? I can't keep up.

Positive self-talk: Since the priority list is flexible, I should divide the task into sections so that if I get distracted, I'll know where to pick up later.

Watch for these other telltale signs of negative thoughts.

Catastrophic Thinking

Negative thought: We'll never finish this project. It's doomed to fail, but what do they expect?

Positive self-talk: We need to find ways to finish this project. They're depending on us.

Negative thought: Things are so bad that I'll probably get demoted by the time the year's up.

➡

Positive self-talk: Things are challenging, but I know we'll find ways to keep up.

Negative thinking: So many employees have left that we'll never be able to replace them. Then what?

Positive self-talk: What are some ways we can attract new employees?

What-If Thinking

Negative thought: What if we don't get approval for this project?

Positive self-talk: We should think of ways to approach this project so we can get approval.

Negative thought: What if we don't have enough time to finish the presentation?

Positive self-talk: We need to manage our time so that we can finish that presentation.

I-Can't-Take-It Thinking

Negative thought: I just can't stand this—I'm overwhelmed.

Positive self-talk: Sure, I've had this much pressure before, and I got through it okay.

Negative thought: I can't take one more e-mail demanding my attention.

Positive self-talk: I'm going to open only the top-priority e-mails today and not look at the others until tomorrow morning.

Part Three

**Perfect Phrases for
Communicating with
Difficult Bosses**

The stress of communicating with a difficult boss ranks high on most employees' anxiety lists. Bosses wield power over their lives, their careers, their financial well-being, and, it seems, everything else. So when the boss turns out to be a bully or simply a well-intended but hopelessly forgetful person, what do you do? Granted, the answer isn't simple, and you can't apply instant solutions. But follow these points and use the perfect phrases, and you might come pretty close. So sit back, relax (really!), and read on.

Your Boss Never Went to Boss School, So Consider Yourself an Employee Management Teacher (Just Don't Tell the Boss)

Most managers, whether in large corporations or family-owned businesses, became bosses because they were experts in the field. Maybe they owned a restaurant and knew how to manage money. Maybe they were trained in a particular area of technical expertise. Regardless, they were not trained to be bosses. Granted, you may be thinking your boss attended an impressive management program or has a sky-high degree. Doesn't count. Most of these programs teach participants how to manage a business, not the people in it.

As a result, even the most professional and well intended of the lot may have trouble communicating with you. And you know what happens from there: You don't get timely information relevant to your job, accurate feedback on your performance so you can improve, or direction on key projects … and worse. So in many cases, you will need to guide the communication with them instead. Take initiative. Ask for what you want. And be specific.

Stick to Names, Tasks, and Agreements—and Steer Clear of Emotions

When communicating with your boss, you may ache to tearfully explain how hard you're trying. How much you value the job. And how terribly unappreciated you really are. Or you may want to proclaim your rights, demand high standards, and tell your boss what you truly think. Try to resist such impulses because even though venting may be great for your emotional well-being (unless it gets you fired), it won't get you far at work.

Instead, focus on *actionable* issues. Did your boss insult you? Put you down at a meeting? Instead of stating you're enraged or hurt, be clear that, as a professional, you expect professional and appropriately timed feedback. Is your boss forcing you to work ridiculous hours without extra compensation? Your boss won't care if you're tired or suffering from workplace fatigue. But remember that employee handbook? That roles and responsibilities agreement? Your boss needs to abide by that. Oh, and does your boss *really* expect you to do a great job when the bags under your eyes are so big you can hardly see? If your work hours are too long too often, your work and your workplace will surely suffer. So discuss that.

You Have Supports—So Use Them

You have more supports than you think when your boss fails you. Some are obvious: manuals, Web site training programs, and online articles to fill in information gaps. Some are available when trouble springs: HR representatives, company psychologists, or resources through your union. Don't forget your coworkers and other colleagues. They may have insights that make your relationship with that difficult boss more productive and relaxed.

Bully Bosses

You never know why bosses bully: Is it their idea of a great management style? Personal problems at home? No metaphorical dog to kick so they come looking for you? In the end, the reason doesn't matter. You have to handle the situation to protect yourself. You deserve and need respect and support at work, especially when projects are complex or overwhelming. These perfect phrases will give you great ideas about how to approach the bully boss and what to say when you do.

How to Confront the Bully Boss

Sure, you may be confronting the person who writes your reviews, gives you raises, and influences your future. But that doesn't mean you should accept this person's insults or attempts to embarrass you around other people. Here are a few starter phrases that can help:

- Comments like that are unproductive and do nothing but create bad feelings.
- Please don't call me, or my ideas, "stupid."
- Comments like that are unprofessional—and against company policy.
- If you have negative feedback about my performance, please give it to me privately.
- Please stop [*name behavior here*].
- I don't appreciate jokes about my spouse or anyone else in my family.
- You must address me by my real name

> *Quick tip:* Be sure to confront your boss privately. A confrontation in front of other people will only embarrass your boss and increase the likelihood that he or she will fight back.

Still Not Getting the Response You Want?

Then try using the *respect-demand order*. When engaging in a conversation with your boss about his or her behavior, using the respect-demand order will start you on a positive and productive footing that establishes a context for the demands ahead. Here is what the respect-demand structure looks like:

Respect　　　Demand

(*respect*) I respect your opinion, (*demand*) but I will not listen to inflammatory comments.

Here are some other examples:

- I would like to improve my performance, but comments like that give me no direction.
- I would like to increase my sales volume, but hearing how bad a job I'm doing doesn't help.
- We all try to provide great customer service, and embarrassing my team in front of the customers destroys our efforts.
- I would like to excel in this company, but hearing that I'm not living up to expectations doesn't give me a sense of direction.

Then be specific about the direction you want:

- I would like to know specific ways I can improve.

➡

- Please let me know what results you expect and how I can recognize them once I've reached them.
- What should I do if that problem comes up again?
- How will I know if I am getting this right?
- What signs of improvement should I look for?
- If I find the situation is getting derailed, what would you like me to do?
- If we confront an emergency, what would you rather we do?

Point Out Repercussions That Actually Hurt the Boss

- Because you yelled at the group, three people have switched teams.
- You may notice that Jay seems dispirited since you ridiculed him in the meeting.
- Since you started calling people "dumb" and "ridiculous," they're not speaking out at the brainstorming sessions.
- After you called our plan "goofy" and other names, I can't get my team to make the deadlines.
- Since the trouble last week, our sales have been down.

Document Your Boss's Behavior

Record your boss's bullying behavior in a file *at home*. Include dates, places, specific comments, and witnesses. And remember to be objective. Here's a reminder of the difference:

Don't use subjective language: The boss yelled really loudly.

Do use objective language: Several people in accounting commented that they heard the boss yelling at me yesterday. He said that I …

➡

Don't use subjective language: The boss was rude.

Do use objective language: Yesterday the boss made several lewd jokes about my wife at the managers' meeting even though I asked him to stop several times. Among other things, he said …

Don't use subjective language: The boss is demoralizing and unfair.

Do use objective language: The boss said the results were "disgusting" and that I am unqualified to do the job, even though I have had high scores from previous bosses.

Don't use subjective language: Every time I walk into the office, the boss makes me feel bad.

Do use objective language: Every time I walk into the office, the boss calls me …

> *Quick tip:* Protect yourself—get support from outside sources, including coworkers who experience the same behavior, the manager who hired you, or even legal counsel.

First Confront Your Boss

- I really value my job here and want to improve. That's why I need to discuss …
- I appreciate your meeting with me. I have a few issues I wanted to bring up because I feel they're interfering with my doing a good job.

➡

- As you know, I try to provide excellent customer service, but something is getting in the way.
- Working here has been a highly positive experience, but I do need to discuss several issues with you.
- I have three issues I'm anxious/eager to resolve with you.
- There are a few problems that I need to discuss with you.

Then Conclude Your Discussion

- Thanks for discussing this with me. I feel much better and look forward to moving on.
- I'm sure this discussion will help me do a better job going forward.
- I appreciate your feedback. I know this will help.
- Please let me know if you have any feedback for me. I always appreciate your insights.
- Thanks for letting me know your views and hearing mine.

Unfocused and Forgetful Bosses

These bosses may be victims of overwhelming schedules or of their own management styles—big picture, visionary, and incapable of seeing details. Regardless, your mission is to help them help you. That means you must control your frustration and put in your own controls. This section provides some perfect phrases that can help.

Start Every Discussion with a Reminder

Sure, your boss is a good person. An expert in the field. And fully capable of managing a great employee like you … if only … he or she could remember your last conversation and the last decision that was made. So you need to remind this boss. Not once, but before starting every discussion. And be discreet—you don't want to embarrass your boss or put your boss on the defensive. Here are some perfect conversation starters:

- After we talked about my taking responsibility for …
- As we discussed last Friday, I am going to compile information about …
- Since you told me to assign Julie responsibility for …
- Clarence has rearranged the plans, as you recommended, but now we need to …
- When we talked last week, you said that we should shift gears and work on …
- In your e-mail, when you said I should train the whole team, were you including …

Refer to Outcomes That Your Manager Expected

- So that each employee participates equally, as you recommended in the managers' meeting, we have reassigned roles and responsibilities.

- The only way for managers to pass the test that you require is for them to receive …

- The results that you intended can happen if we …

- To reach your goal of … we need to …

- Everyone thinks your goal of … is a great idea. To make that happen, we're proposing …

- So we can hire the right employees and ramp up quickly, as you stated in your project meeting last week …

Show Results, Offer Actions, and Keep It Positive

Make sure your results are positive and in line with your boss's goals. Notice the difference between negative and positive positioning:

Negative: We'll miss our deadlines for the client's proposal unless you assign Larry to our team.

Positive: We'll be sure to make our deadlines for the client's proposal if you assign Larry to our team.

Negative: We won't get our budget the same as last year unless we …

Positive: We can get our budget and perform the same as last year if we …

Negative: Our customer rating will never improve unless we add the new …

Positive: Our customer rating can improve if we add the new …

Show Results, Offer Actions, and Keep It Specific

General: Marcie can really contribute to this project, so I'd like to …

Specific: Marcie can contribute financial expertise to the project, so I'd like to …

General: We can expedite processes if we …

Specific: We can get the product from the factory to the warehouse 25 percent faster if we …

General: We can get a great return on our investment if we …

Specific: We can possibly increase profits by 40 percent if we …

Remind Your Boss of His or Her Previous Instructions

If something goes wrong because you were following instructions but your boss blames you for it, remind your boss about what he or she requested you to do—and forgot:

- In your e-mail on Friday, you said that I should …
- I was following your instructions from the team meeting.
- In your office, you changed the project plan and assigned me that responsibility, and you said David should …
- Because Sherrie had to go on leave, you said I should take over. You also recommended that I …

If your boss gives you an assignment but then assigns someone else the task when you're halfway through, here are some ways for you to get back on track. For example, if you have had great results and want to continue with the project, show the results *first:*

- I have the results that you asked for in January. Do you want me to continue with this project, or should Hector take over?
- So far, I've … I'd like to continue if that's okay.
- My next step is to … Should I continue?
- I assembled the team and drafted a project management plan. Now that I have some momentum, I'd like to keep going.

If your boss seems hesitant about allowing you to remain with it or if the project won't be jeopardized if you leave it, finish your statement by offering to move on (or back) to something else:

- If you like, I can continue with the … that I started in May.
- I can put this on hold if you want me to.
- At this point, Larry can take over and we won't lose any momentum.
- I haven't talked to the clients yet, so they have no expectations. If you want Julie to jump in, the transition should be smooth.
- If you want me to stop, I can.
- I can always give my notes to the team and go back to the other project.
- If you like, I can give the update in the meeting. I know the subject well, and that way, you won't have to prepare anything.

> *Quick tip:* Write down your boss's instructions so that you can refer to them later. Did the boss give you instructions on the fly? Mention them at a meeting? Write them down and e-mail them to everyone involved. And yes, send a copy to the boss. Always.

Distant, Weak, or Hands-Off Bosses

So you have a distant, hands-off boss. Your boss provides little support and tends to have the backbone of a jellyfish. Is the problem your boss's personality? Is he or she burned out? Too introverted to confront problem employees or difficult clients? Maybe your boss just wants to be liked and shies away from anything contentious.

While you don't want to psychoanalyze your boss, answering these questions can help you get better results. For example, if you know your boss has checked out of the job and is in maintenance mode, you should probably get support from others in your unit. If your boss is overwhelmed, then work together to find solutions.

Give Your Boss Ideas

- For the next phase of this project, I'd like to …
- Last year, we used a strategy that worked really well, and I'd like to use it again. It is …
- I was thinking about the project and had some great ideas.
- I know we're having problems with this project. Here are a few things I think would help.
- Actually, the problems we're having are typical of other companies in our industry. I found these best practices that could be helpful to us.
- I talked to a few people on our team and came up with some really great ideas.

> *Quick tip:* Focus on the positive results you'll get—not the problems you want to avoid.

Make Sure You Get Your Boss to Say Yes

Follow your ideas with phrases like these:

- Does that sound good to you?
- Do I have your okay to move forward?
- Do you think this is a good idea?
- Does that sound like a reasonable approach?
- This seems workable, don't you agree?
- Will you give me your consent to move forward?
- Okay if I get started right away?
- I want to get moving on this immediately. Is that all right with you?
- As long as you feel comfortable with this, I'll get started, okay?

> *Quick tip:* Ask your boss if you should take additional steps or consider additional factors. That way, you'll engage your boss in the discussion, and he or she will have greater ownership of the task and will be more likely to support you as you go.

Request Specific Actions When You Need Support

- Do you think you could remind the project leader that we need the content by Friday?
- Could you please talk to Matt? He refuses to get us the data we need, and we can't move ahead with the project.
- Would you check Gail's agenda before the client meeting so that we can avoid the problems we experienced last year?

When Possible, Offer to Do Some of the Work

- Can you please correct the vendor's mistake on the purchase order? I can e-mail you the problem with his calculation and indicate the correct amount.

- Could you let the team members know they really need to attend the wrap-up meetings on Friday mornings? I can e-mail you a statement that you can send.

- The lobby has been a mess lately. If it's okay, can I draft a request from you saying that maintenance should do a better job cleaning?

Establish a Realistic—and Specific—Way to Get Direction and Feedback

- Can our team meet every Monday morning to make plans for the week ahead?

- Can you meet with our customer service reps once a month to review the feedback?

- I have this project management sheet. Do you think you could fill in the comments section? Then I'll pass it along to the team.

- Can you tell Roz the outcome of the meeting? Then she can e-mail it to all of us.

- Perhaps John should come to the senior managers' meeting. Then he can pass on the information to all of us.

- If you could post changes on the department bulletin board every Monday, we will review them.

- We would all appreciate your walking around the floor once or twice a week and giving us feedback on our customer service.

Ask Your Boss Directly for Support with a Difficult Customer

1. Provide Background

- The customer claimed the bill was wrong, but that was because she missed the sale date.
- The customer's boss put in one request and the customer changed it. Now the customer claims we didn't send the right shipment.
- The clients are upset because they thought our report didn't have enough substance.

2. Show Outcome

- We want to resolve this with her.
- We want to get them the right product as soon as possible.
- We want them to know we value them and will fill in the holes.

3. Request an Action

- Can you waive the sale date so that we can give her the discount?
- Could you please contact the customers to confirm that the order is correct?

➡

- Could you call the CEO and apologize to him and assure him that we'll correct this mistake?

Ask Your Boss Directly for Support with a Difficult Coworker

- Would you please define Gail's specific role in this project?
- Could you remind Juanita the she shouldn't have direct contact with the client?
- Would you mind confirming the schedule with Tom before we start the project?
- Could you e-mail our team the steps you want us to take? I can send the ones you originally gave us.
- We have received complaints that John monopolizes meetings with the client. Can you meet with him on Monday to discuss this issue?

How to Ask for an Overdo Promotion or Raise

Before asking for that promotion or raise, make sure you really deserve one. Or, more to the point, make sure you can *prove* you deserve it. How long have you been with the company? What tasks are you able to fulfill that make you more valuable than when you were first hired? What level are other employees with your skills, longevity, and background? Once you have gathered the evidence, then approach the boss. Here are some phrases that will help.

Start By Saying What You Like about Your Job

- I really enjoy working here, especially all the challenges involved in …

- I really enjoy working with customers …

- As you already know, I really appreciate all the opportunities I've had working here.

- Working here has been a wonderful experience, especially …

- Since I've been here, I've had a range of experiences that have helped me grow professionally, such as …

Add Any Personal Factors

- For the past five years that I've been here, …
- My experience has ranged from …
- I have put in some long weeks—often 50 or 55 hours.
- I have worked with clients in every area.
- During this time, I have received a master's degree.

State Why You Want the Raise or Promotion

Remember to keep it professional—not personal:

Personal: My husband and I want to buy a new house and need additional income.

Professional: I feel I am able to contribute more as a …

Personal: I really feel like I deserve more money than I'm getting.

Professional: Given my new responsibilities, I feel that I provide greater value to the company.

Personal: Everyone tells me that I should get more money for all the work I do.

Professional: Given the amount of extra time I put in, …

Accent the Value of Your Role

By "role" you mean your position. Be sure to elaborate on extra responsibilities or areas of expertise that may enhance your value to your company:

- My role has become increasingly important as we …
- As an account manager, my role now includes overseeing …
- Although I am responsible for … my role also entails …
- I was originally hired to do … Now my role also requires that I …
- According to my job description, I should … But now I also oversee …

Accent Your Personal Value

- I am fluent in three languages, which is helpful when international customers come in.
- I am also certified in …
- I have had training in project management, which has helped me …
- My training as an engineer gives me a firm grasp of …
- As you know, I have a quick learning curve. For example, I was able to learn the … , which helped us …
- My 10 years living abroad has given me experience in establishing relationships with people in foreign cultures, so I can …

Quick tip: As the old saying goes, "Timing is everything." So don't ask your boss for a raise just after a catastrophe has hit your unit—even if you scheduled the appointment well in advance.

Discuss How You'll Continue to Help Your Organization Grow

- Given my experience, I can help the sales department reach new markets.
- I know most of our top clients quite well. This will enable us to …
- If I were to work in that position, I could devote more time to …
- As a … , I could help the company reach the goals of … This is how: …

➡

- As part of the … team, I could fill in a missing component of our leadership. This will help us reach several key goals, including …
- I spent three years in that position in my former job. I could bring that experience and expertise …

Use One of These Responses If Your Boss Turns Down Your Request

- Can you tell me what I need to do to get that promotion?
- I am really interested in moving ahead here. What can you recommend that I do?
- What do most people accomplish before they get a raise?
- Can you think of ways I can improve my performance?
- Can you recommend any courses or additional training that would make me right for the job?

Quick tip: Don't threaten to resign or look elsewhere … unless you mean it. And before you resign, make sure jobs are available first!

Micromanagers

No mere sticklers for detail, micromanagers can be obsessed. Maybe they bully you. Maybe they batter you. Or possibly they're oh-so friendly and polite. Regardless, they treat you as if you were 12. But don't take it personally. Just be glad you're not married to them and learn how *you* can manage *them*. Your best bet: a proactive style and an eye to ongoing communication that helps them feel in control. And pick your battles carefully: Micromanagers are known to find fault. Don't worry or quibble about the little issues; just make changes (however unnecessary) and move on. Here are some other tips that will help and perfect phrases as you go.

Assure the Boss That You're Ahead on the Details, Even When the Boss Doesn't Ask

- I contacted Mr. Smiley to get his approval.
- I reviewed the statistics, and all of them have been updated.
- I checked the inventory against last year's figures.

When Possible, Connect This Action to Something Your Boss Previously Recommended to Give Your Boss a Feeling of Control

- As you required last year, I …
- I followed the same procedure you established last time.
- Before, you wanted us to … I did this again.

Provide Information at the Outset—Don't Wait to Be Asked

- I called the office, and they said the deadline will be two days earlier this year.

➡

- I reviewed the regulation and found that it doesn't require us to …

- When I spoke to Ms. Sealy, I asked her about …

- I found out that the biggest reason companies get turned down for the program is that …

- I researched this a little and found that most experts think the best action plan is to …

Stay in Touch

- Just wanted to update you about our progress so far.

- I am sending along a task list so that you can review our progress, if you like.

- I'm attaching feedback from the most recent customer survey. I'll compile all the responses for our meeting in March.

- At the managers' meeting, I'd like to update everyone about our progress, if you think that's appropriate.

- If you want a short meeting so that I can update you about the project, just let me know.

> *Quick tip:* Pick your methods of communication carefully. Some micromanagers double as control freaks (no surprise!), and they may feel overwhelmed by a volume of e-mail they can't control. Others may have bad memories and won't remember one word of what you say to them in person; they rely on the written word.

Give Your Boss an Opportunity to Provide Feedback or Direction

Even if he or she doesn't routinely take the initiative to give feedback or direction (which is ideal!), your boss will feel in control and will more likely leave you alone if you seek his or her opinion frequently:

- Does this idea sound good to you?
- Do you have any thoughts about our current direction?
- Does this seem like the best method to you?

Frame Your Requests to Presuppose a Thumbs-Up

- Last year you said that we should … so I'm going to follow your advice again.
- This is the same process we used last year, and it improved our delivery time by three days. Shall we use it again?
- I think this was originally your strategy. With your approval, I'd like to use it again.

Create Structure Around Your Project—and Get Your Boss to Agree

- I think we can complete Step 1 by the fifteenth and Step 2 by the twentieth. Does that sound good to you?
- I worked up a short project plan for your approval.
- Here is our updated timetable. As you can see, we're right on track. Should we continue?
- I have a list of everyone's responsibilities for this project and his or her goals. Do you want to change anything, or does the list look okay?
- I'm using the same schedule that we used for a similar project last year. Does this look good to you?

> *Quick tip:* Don't be afraid to show initiative. Even if your boss turns you down, he or she will still feel a sense of power and will respect you for taking extra initiative.

Help the Boss Feel in Control

Use questions rather than statements so that your micromanaging boss can actively participate in the discussion and feel a greater sense of control:

Statement: I'd like to get your input.

Question: Do you have any input?

Statement: I am interested in reading about this subject.

Question: Can you recommend any articles for me to read?

Statement: I hope you're happy with the changes.

Question: Are you happy with these changes?

Know the Rule Book?

Follow it—and let your manager know that you are:

- As the regulation requires, we have …
- In your memo, you said that we should … As you can see, we followed your instructions completely.
- These are the best practices you outlined last week. We have applied them to solving this problem.

➡

- As you know, we are required to ... So we have ...
- The CEO stated that we need to reach each of these goals by ...

> *Quick tip:* Document, document, document and remember to bring your notes to the meeting.

How to Correct Your Boss's Mistakes

Yes, it can be embarrassing to correct your boss's mistakes, depending on the boss. While some see themselves as fallible human beings and don't mind that everyone knows it, others want to be perceived as gods. They always have to be right, and they'll throw a bolt of lightning at anyone who says they're wrong. The reason? In a word: ego. So how do you protect your boss's ego without letting him or her play you for the fool? *And* how do you position yourself as a valuable and irreplaceable contributor? Read on.

Broach the Subject

- I'm not sure if you realized this, but …
- Are you aware that …
- The presentation that you gave was right on the mark. Just two facts I wanted to point out …
- Just so you know, I wanted to point out that …
- You may not be aware that you said … when you probably meant …
- Normally, we take these steps … Are you thinking you want to change them?
- The report usually includes … But not … Should we stick with the old way, or do you want to change it?

Compliment Your Boss

It's always nice to compliment your boss when discussing his or her mistake. Think of it as a verbal Valium to soothe humiliation. Here's what you can say:

- Everyone knows you're an expert in

➡

- Because you know the information so well, this detail probably slipped by.
- Because you're so busy, it's hard for you to remember the names of everyone in the room.
- We know you're better versed in this than any of us.
- Given the fact you have a master's degree and a Ph.D., you're clearly ahead in that subject.
- Because you're a big-picture visionary, you're bound to miss the details.

Suggest Ways to Avoid the Mistake in the Future

- We have forms so that you or your assistant can document everything you said at the meeting. These might help you remember …
- I was thinking about the meeting yesterday and had a few ideas. Would you like to hear them?
- I read in an article about … that can help us with …
- I know that other managers have overcome issues like these by …
- According to *Time* magazine [*or other publication, Web site, or authority*], most managers have to address issues like this constantly. Would you like me to get you the article?

Quick tip: When making suggestions, rely on facts, information you gleaned from articles, or your own experience or the experience of others. While you have the best intentions, be careful about how you make your points so that your boss won't think you're overbearing or trying to usurp his or her authority.

Follow up with offers to double check similar reports, statements, or facts your boss got wrong. This has lots of advantages: Your boss will appreciate the offer, will have the power to accept (or reject) your offer and maintain a leadership position, and will value you for giving the extra help.

Follow Up with an Offer the Boss Can't Refuse

Not: You're not a detail person, so I had better check these numbers.

But: I have a really keen eye for detail. If you like, I can check those numbers.

Not: So you don't embarrass yourself again in front of our customers, I can check your speaking points.

But: Most professionals get second opinions on those speaking points. Would you like me to review them in the future?

Here are a few others:

- Because I have had a great deal of experience in …
- I really enjoy proofreading. If you like, I can proofread your newsletter pieces.
- In my old position, I … for my boss all the time. Would you like me to … for you too?
- I have a degree in that subject so I know it well. If you like, I can review those points before you submit them.
- I would really enjoy reviewing those before you submit them.
- If you like, I can give the update in the meeting. I know the subject well, and that way, you won't have to prepare anything.

How to Get a Letter of Recommendation from a Reluctant Boss

Getting a letter of recommendation can be embarrassing for even the best employees—with the easiest boss. For starters, you don't want to give your boss extra work. And, in a way, you're asking for compliments. Who feels comfortable with that? Besides, what if you and the boss have a rocky relationship? Well, don't be afraid, embarrassed, or reluctant. Just use these perfect phrases.

State Why You Want the Letter of Recommendation

Explain why you are seeking a letter of recommendation even if it is for another job but especially if it's for a professional or academic program you wish to pursue:

- As you know, I have been helping our clients with their accounting systems, and I think this course will help me with that work.

- By going to graduate school, I'll be able to excel in the organization. For example, …

- This course provides information that will directly support our work on the …

- The connection between the information I'll get in this program and the direction our sales department is taking is strong.

- This program supports my performance objective of …

- I'll learn strategies that will support our mission of …

> *Quick tip:* The more specific you are about how the program will improve your performance, the better. So avoid lines like "This program will help me be a better employee," and focus on specific benefits for your employer.

State That Your Recommendation Will Be Easy to Complete

- I just need a paragraph or two.
- If you could fill out this one-page recommendation form, ...
- All they need to know is what I have achieved professionally.
- They need to know only about my accomplishments, and most of those were listed in my recent performance review.
- If you can let them know about my work on the ... project and my accomplishments with ... that would be great.
- They need only a letter—three paragraphs at most.
- If you like, I can send you a letter of recommendation a past employer drafted for me.
- I have a sample recommendation form. Would you like me to send it?

Request a Recommendation Even If You and Your Boss Have Had a Rocky Road

If you think your boss may not want to give you a recommendation for some reason, you can still ask for one if you frame your request with the facts and nothing but the facts:

➡

- During my time here, my team has increased sales by 20 percent in the first quarter, and 15 percent each quarter after that.
- As you know, I have had numerous successes, including …
- As an employee for almost 10 years, I have contributed to several key initiatives, including …
- I have received awards for … and commendations from …
- I was the first employee to apply the … and I helped implement the software system that employees rely on today.
- Thanks to my analysis, the company saved over $100,000 a year on cycle time issues.
- I have an excellent rapport with our customers, especially Ben and Sylvia, whom I talk to almost every day.

Offer to Send Points, Highlight Key Projects, or Write the Recommendation Yourself

- If you like, I can send a list of my accomplishments for you to include.
- I can write up a quick list of points they need to know.
- I can send along key points from my performance review. Since you wrote them, you may only need to approve them.
- I can write the letter and then send it in for your approval.
- I'd be happy to draft a letter of recommendation for you, if you like.
- To make it easy, I can outline the points for the letter and give examples of major projects.

➡

Quick tip: Yes, you will need to discuss your personal attributes—you know, how great you are with people, how responsive, proactive, and intelligent. You know the list. But be sure to follow each claim with a specific example. This will turn a claim into a fact. Here a few examples:

Claim: She gets along well with our customers.

Fact: We regularly receive e-mails of appreciation from customers, and she received two awards from our company complimenting her skills.

Claim: She comes up with unique ideas.

Fact: She proposed applying a knowledge management system from 10 years ago to solving our problem with … As a result, we were able to …

Claim: He is proactive.

Fact: Two years ago, he helped us avoid costly problems by anticipating cash flow problems and …

How to Say Good-bye to a Problem Boss—Without Burning Bridges

Start By Saying Something Positive about the Job

Be specific:

- As you know, I've been here for three years. I feel I have learned a great deal from working here.
- This has been one of the best experiences of my professional life. I really learned an incredible amount from …
- The variety of positions I've held here has given me amazing insights into …
- I really appreciate all the wonderful opportunities I've had here, especially …
- When I started, I was a … In only two years, I have grown to become …

Then Explain Why You're Leaving

- I need to grow further professionally, and while I enjoy working here, I would benefit from …
- The company's new direction will require different areas of expertise than what I enjoy doing.
- I need to find new challenges.
- The company has changed a great deal recently, and I feel like the match isn't as good as it once was.
- I've decided to take a different direction professionally.

Give the Boss as Many Options as Possible to Make the Transition Easy

- I was hoping to leave by mid-October, but I have flexibility if you need me to stay longer.

➥

- What is a good date for me to leave?
- I'll be happy to stay until the end of the year.
- I can wait until I complete this project so I don't leave you or my coworkers stuck.
- If you like, I can stay on part time for a few weeks.
- Even though I need to move on in two weeks, I will be available after hours to answer any questions through e-mail, and I will check my voice mail throughout the day.
- I'm going to leave all my notes and updates to the project plans for my replacement. He or she can call with questions at any time.

Suggest Future Relations

- I am planning to go into consulting. I'll let you know when my business is up and running.
- I'd like to continue working on part-time projects. Would you like me to get in touch in a few weeks?
- I'll keep you updated as I move on.
- Please let me know how things are going here. As you know, everyone here is like a family to me.
- I'll be working from home and always welcome projects I can do from there.
- Maybe we can work on joint projects in the future.
- If I meet anyone who could use your services, I'll definitely send him or her your way.

Thank Your Boss Personally

Again, be specific:

- Thanks for all your time—especially for mentoring me in the first few weeks.

- I really appreciate all the risks you took in giving me new work.
- I know you bailed me out quite a few times. Thanks. I learned an incredible amount from the experience.
- You really taught me how to work as part of a team. I'll take that with me into my next job.

> *Quick tip:* Let the last good-bye be a *good* bye. You know the saying that "first impressions are lasting impressions"? In this case, the last impressions last the longest. Make sure your boss has a positive impression as you make your exit even if you didn't get along. Send a thank-you card. Invite your boss to lunch once you've left. Or at the very least, seal your exit with a handshake—a firm one. And really mean it.

Part Four

Perfect Phrases for Communicating with Difficult Employees

L et's face it, you probably were never taught how to communicate with employees. Or if you were, the lessons were ludicrously general like how to distinguish between an introvert's and an extrovert's communication style. But how did this information translate into words you should use when an employee smells so bad it distracts anyone who walks into the office. Or how to get a passive-aggressive employee to do what he or she has been asked to do. The answer, of course, is that it didn't help you at all. And you, unfortunately, are left to wing it or, even worse, say nothing at all.

Well, you've come to the right place. In this part of the book, you'll find plenty of information about how to use communication *not* as a Band-Aid but as a true management tool for getting results. As you turn the pages, keep these principles in mind:

- *Focus on actions, not attitudes.* If you are like most managers, you would probably love to see a happy workplace—employees smiling, bobbing around as if on a pleasure cruise. But that rarely happens—even on actual cruise ships. Instead, employees' problems often become problems for everyone around them. To manage your problems with employees effectively, focus on their actions rather than on their demeanors or attitudes. Don't worry if an employee is sullen behind the scenes. If he or she provides great customer service and gives you complete reports on time, that's what counts. When an employee's actions are less than perfect, you need to comment on that specific performance, not on the emotion that could be fueling it.

- *Timing may not be everything … but it sure helps.* When you communicate with an employee matters. If the employee dropped the ball, e-mail or talk to him or her when the ball is still on the ground—not days or weeks later. Make sure you communicate in the right setting also. A quiet, confidential office is usually better than a confrontation in a meeting or public area. And remember that even if you're talking softly, body language screams.

- *Timing also applies to the* number *of times you speak to an employee.* While one time should do it, it usually doesn't. Most employees have trouble retaining spoken requests regardless of how clear you are. So you should follow up with an e-mail and, for more important matters, a face-to-face conversation once or twice.

- *Keep your eyes, and your employees' eyes, on the prize.* At work, the prize may be a better parking space, pay hike, or bonus. But it also needs to be something else: something greater, more enduring, and more connected to your employees' having fulfilling work lives. In other words, your employees need to have a strong sense of the value of their work. Maybe your company makes customers' lives safer. Perhaps it makes them happier somehow. Or maybe it gives them a benefit that affects their wallets every time they make a purchase. Focus your employees on that.

Complainers

Constant complaints rank as one of your most formidable foes. They undermine morale, slow productivity, and foster negativity that is contagious. One negative employee, supervisor, or even contractor can start a virus that spreads throughout your organization. You can't tell your employee to lighten up, take a more positive outlook, or get a grip. And you don't want to sound like a Pollyanna, forcing fake rays of sun into your employee's discontent. Instead, make yourself available to address the complaints, using these phrases.

Show That You're Listening

- Thanks for letting me know your impression.
- I appreciate your input.
- I understand what you mean.
- I was not aware that you saw the situation that way.
- That's an interesting way of seeing the situation.
- Thanks for giving me your take on that matter.

> *Quick tip:* Don't use highly negative or catastrophic wording because it will only reinforce your employee's negativity and block your ability to get past it.

Validate the Employee's Concerns

If you agree with the comments, let the employee know immediately. This will validate the employee and lower his or her defensiveness. Also, indicate how you—or the employee—will move ahead:

- I agree with many of your points. Let's discuss ways we can address them.
- You're right in saying … What do you think we should do?
- Much of what you're saying has validity; so let's clarify some of the points.
- Yes, I agree. Actually, I'm meeting with the board on Friday to discuss this issue.
- I think you're right about some of those points. Let me update you about what we're doing.

Be Diplomatic

When you disagree, be diplomatic. Otherwise, you might embarrass the employee, make him or her feel you weren't attentive, or otherwise fuel the negativity.

Avoid Saying Things Like These

- You're wrong.
- That is ridiculous.
- I don't think any other employee sees it that way.
- Well, you must have blinders on.
- Where did you ever get that impression?
- I cannot imagine why you're complaining.
- I think you have it good.
- Then try working somewhere else.

Instead, Discuss Objective Evidence That Proves Your Point

- Actually, the meeting notes indicate that what I actually said was …

➡

- According to your contract, you can only …
- I have the e-mail that I sent, and as you will see if you look in your mailbox, what I actually said was …
- The manual requires that we take those steps to avoid …
- Actually, we conducted a survey of … which revealed that …
- Our customers indicated that they would prefer if we …

Maintain Control

Avoid letting the employee put you on the defensive:

- Instead of arguing the point, let's look at steps to move forward.
- So what do you think is the solution?
- I understand your point. Now what other matters did you want to discuss?
- At this point, you need be clear about a solution, not only the problem.

How to Take a Forward-Looking Approach

Employee comment: The projects keep changing. How can you expect me to get anything done?

Forward-looking response: Let's look at what's on the agenda now and work up an action plan.

Employee comment: No one here knows what's necessary for the project but me. And I can't do everything myself, especially with this tight deadline.

Forward-looking response: So what are some ways we can get people caught up? How else can we support you?

Other Forward-Looking Phrases

- Every situation has downsides, I agree. Now tell me what you think we can do about them.
- Given those circumstances, here are the results we should focus on achieving.
- Let's look at the goals we can reach at this point.
- Regardless of those issues, we still have a mission to fulfill, so let's figure out the best way to get there.
- We'll address each of those issues when they come up.
- Okay, now let's look for solutions to those problems.
- We've addressed each of those drawbacks in previous projects, so we have plenty of solutions we can apply.

Give the Employee the Power

Give your employee responsibility for finding solutions. Be specific about how to do that:

- Why not think up three or four ideas, e-mail me, and we can talk again next week.
- If you want to discuss this further, think up some ways of addressing these complaints and e-mail them to me.
- Please e-mail me a plan that will resolve this problem with some time frames attached to every phase.
- I'd like you to draft a list of these concerns and write solutions beside each of them. Then, let's discuss possibilities on Tuesday at 8:00.
- In spite of these issues, tasks really do get done—on time and with great feedback from our clients. So I'd like you to find ways you can personally improve or live with them.

- We're known for having some of the best problem solvers in our field. So I'm sure you can solve each of the concerns you've raised.

> *Quick tip:* Are the complaints fostering a negative environment? If so, discuss the effects of negativity and remind your employees to take a more productive approach. Perhaps invite a specialist for a brown bag lunch or half-day seminar on how to protect against negative messages and resist conveying them. This will help difficult employees use more positive language. It will also create social pressure to make difficult employees resist griping and show fellow employees how to approach negativity when they confront it.

How to Address Inappropriate Behavior, Dress, or Hygiene

One of the most embarrassing and difficult issues for any manager is addressing an employee's personal affectation. The matter isn't exactly personal … or professional, making it uncomfortably ambiguous. Whether you should address the matter at all depends on numerous factors. To find out, ask these questions:

- Does this behavior interfere with work?
- Do other employees complain about it?
- Would the standard for this one employee apply to all the others?
- Is this a one-time event or part of a pattern?
- Do any company policies support the view that the behavior needs to change?

If your answer is yes to some or all of the preceding questions, then proceed with the following steps.

Record Patterns

If an employee makes a rude comment or comes to work inappropriately dressed one time, keep your eyes open afterward but don't address the issue yet. But if the employee shows patterns of inappropriate dress, behavior, or hygiene, keep a clear and objective record:

- Carolyn came to work on Tuesday, Wednesday, and Thursday at 10:00 although she was scheduled to start at 8:00. I spoke with her about this problem on February 10 and 14. She arrived on time for one week, then lapsed into the previous pattern.

- Ed used expletives three times in the meeting on Friday. I spoke with him afterward and sent him a follow-up e-mail. This is the third time this has occurred.
- Although I clearly addressed the company policy about dress in our meeting, James has come to work wearing sandals for two weeks. His team did not feel his clothing was appropriate for the meeting with our client.
- Elena has left work two to three hours early numerous times over the past few months. I discussed this issue with her several times. ... See e-mails.

Quick tip: If sexual harassment or a racial slur was involved even once, take action.

Speak with the Employee in a Quiet, Closed-Door Discussion

Start by mentioning the employee's value to your organization:

- We really value your contributions to all our projects, such as ...
- You are one of our brightest employees.
- I feel that you have enormous potential, and I want to be a mentor for you.
- You have a clear grasp of the issues facing our clients. I think you can go far in the company.
- You are unique among our employees, and you offer the company a great deal.

Then explain that you're mentioning the issue because you want the employee to excel and don't want anything to get in the way:

- I want to ensure that you continue to be effective, so I need to address this matter.
- If you are to continue growing, you need to resolve one matter.
- One issue is standing in the way of your progress. Once you address it, I think your future looks strong.
- My hope is that you remain a critical part of the company. For that to occur, though, …
- I would like to see you … However, one issue is getting in the way.
- To ensure that you work well with other employees, I need to tell you that …
- To help you maintain your professionalism and credibility, …

If discussing hygiene or another sensitive issue, feel free to admit that the discussion makes you uncomfortable:

- I have to admit, I don't feel comfortable telling you this.
- This is a somewhat personal issue—I feel funny discussing it.
- Normally, I don't like discussing personal issues, but this one is important.
- I'm not exactly sure how to put this, but …
- I hope I'm being clear when I say …
- Please don't take offense if I have trouble explaining this, but …

Discuss the Problem

If mentioning that other people have complained, respect their confidentiality and do not name names or even the number of people who have complained. A vague word like *several* or *some* should suffice:

- Several people have commented that an odor is coming from your cubicle.
- You have been wearing sandals and shorts to work, which goes against company policy.
- Several people from bookkeeping have complained that your voice is so loud that they can hear you down the hall.
- Please remember to dress professionally—clean, ironed clothes, shirt tucked in, and shoelaces tied.
- We can smell the cologne the moment we open the office door.
- Several customers have complained that you're yelling at them.

Quick tip: Don't diagnose the problem by, for example, saying "Your clothes are dirty" or present a solution by, for example, saying "You need to shower more often." Instead, give clear and objective evidence that the problem exists; the employee will know what to do.

Indicate How the Behavior Affects Everyone Else

- Your team members feel hesitant about taking you to meetings.

- Five customers have complained so far, and we don't want to lose their business.
- This is distracting at meetings.
- Several people have complained that your approach intimidates them and they can't provide important input.
- Several employees have stated that they find your comments offensive.
- Some participants in the sessions have said your clothing is distracting.

> *Quick tip:* You may need to speak with the employee one or two more times. Still don't get a result? Find the situation worsens? Then contact HR.

Try These Other Phrases Too

When an Employee Does Not Dress Properly

- We have clear policies about dress. You can find them in the employee handbook or contact HR.
- So that we can be effective in our presentations, you need to dress in professional clothing—not shorts or jeans.
- Several employees have commented on the fact that your style of dress may not be reflecting our unit. In particular, you have worn …

When an Employee's Behavior Is Disruptive or Insulting

- The company does not allow name-calling, insults, and imitations. Yet last week, several employees commented that you made disparaging remarks about members of the team including … This must stop immediately.

- In the last meeting, you used swear words when describing your feelings about the project. This is a professional environment, and you need to eliminate these words from your work-life vocabulary.
- You must keep your voice at a pitch sufficiently low that no one can hear you beyond a few feet of your desk.
- During the meeting, you came and went three separate times. Please do not do that again because entering and exiting a meeting in that way is disruptive and distracting to everyone else.

When an Employee Has Hygiene Problems

- Numerous employees have commented on a smell emanating from your office.
- We need to be sure that all offices are clean and organized to ensure that everyone can work as effectively as possible.
- In the last few meetings, several people noticed an odor from the area where you were sitting.

Remember, too, that as a supervisor, if you identify abuse of any kind, you *must* take action. You can speak separately to the offending employee or engage the victim, if he or she feels comfortable.

> *Quick tip:* If an employee has body odor, tread lightly. He or she may be suffering from an illness or be on medication that causes the smell. Should personal cleanliness be the culprit, be aware that depression or a related issue may be involved.

Employees Who Spread Rumors

Contending with gossipy employees may not seem like a management issue, but it is. Gossip can create an environment of insecurity, sever professional relationships, and foster negativity. It can even create confusion over work issues. So you need to address gossip at the source. Here are some ways to do it.

Set a Precedent

Take a moment in a meeting, write a group e-mail, or do both in which you outline the negative effects of gossip mongering:

- You may have heard rumors about changes in the organization. Unless you hear something directly from me, please ignore them. Otherwise, you may be seriously misled.
- Spreading rumors about people is destructive and lacks integrity. So don't do it.
- If you hear rumors about people, ignore them. If you hear someone insulting someone else, insist that the person stop.
- Beware of rumors about promotions. Unless you hear directly from me, they're pure conjecture.
- Remember the old saying "Loose lips sink ships"? Well, that applies to rumors too.

Be Unequivocal

Address rumors immediately—in e-mails or meetings, whichever is fastest:

- We have not announced changes in positions yet.
- You have been receiving inaccurate information about our profits—the year-end reports aren't even in yet.

➡

- Our CEO has not resigned—and no one has suggested that she will.
- If the company were planning to have layoffs, I would be the first to know, and you would be the second.
- Unless information comes from a credible source, don't believe it.

Keep Employees in the Information Loop

The more information employees have from you, the less power workplace gossip will have:

- When we have information, we will notify your manager, who will notify you.
- Please check the intranet regularly for updates. You will be the first to receive them.
- We expect the board to announce its decisions on Friday. We will notify our employees before contacting the media.
- Please look on the portal every day. We will post all information about our unit there before the rest of the organization learns it.
- We have a clear process for informing employees of company information. Look on the intranet if you have questions.
- We will hold regular updates every Monday morning.

Quick tip: If rumors are flying, set up an alert system via meetings or e-mail by which to disseminate information quickly should real changes break. Give these messages or meetings a name or description like "Instant Updates" or "Inside Reports." Employees will learn to get information there—and ignore the rest.

Use These Phrases When the Rumors Are Personal

- Spreading rumors about individuals is unethical and mean-spirited. Please resist doing it.
- Gossip is the lowest form of communication—and as professionals, we are above that.
- If you hear someone gossiping or condemning another person, you owe it to your team to turn away from that gossip.
- Gossip and rude comments about anyone in this organization are among the most destructive forms of communication. So don't engage in it.

> *Quick tip:* Be alert to *mobbing*—that is, when employees gang up on a coworker, manager, or other person. If this is occurring in your workplace, you will need to establish clear standards and rules of conduct to stop such mobbing in all its manifestations.

Lazy or Lethargic Employees

Employees can be lazy or lethargic for countless reasons from being bored with the job to having a lazy disposition. To motivate them, you need to think clarity and carrots. *Clarity*, of course, means asserting a clear vision of the future and a sense of purpose. As for *carrots*? You might think that carrots are rewards such as bonuses, awards, and a good parking space. True, they are, but generally, these rewards are temporary, and once the employees have them, the rewards lose their power. Effective carrots must be more powerful, ongoing, and connected to the value of the jobs they are meant to reward. These carrots are intangible, which means that you must rely on strong communication so that employees can recognize them. This section provides several perfect phrases that will help.

Create Clear, Ongoing Goals

You can achieve this by using the following sentence structure:

Action   Details   Outcome

(action) You must respond to all customer phone calls *(details)* within one hour *(outcome)* to receive 90-plus scores on responsiveness.

Here are more examples:

- You must compile the data at least two days before the quarterly meetings so that we have the material on time and the decision-making process goes as smoothly as planned.
- You must anticipate the customers' difficulties by getting them solutions within 24 hours which will cut costs associated with emergency follow-up by at least 10 percent.

- By getting the information into the report when you draft it, you can expedite the decision-making process by at least two days.

You can move that order around too:

Outcome   Action   Details

- (*outcome*) You can increase employee morale and lower the volume of inquiries (*action*) by drafting regular updates about (*details*) …
- (*outcome*) So that you can help increase our industry rating, (*action*) you need to complete the following actions 100 percent of the time: (*details*) …

Quick tip: Keep your goals *real* and specific so that they have meaning for lethargic employees. And avoid empty phrases like these:

- Meet our customer's needs
- Provide superior customer service
- Become a leader in …
- Be known as the leading …
- Customize our service
- Be there when our customer needs us
- Be a true partner with our client

Follow Up

Determine how a lethargic employee failed or succeeded even when the measurements aren't immediately transparent:

- Since you have been getting the reports out on time, our average customer response time has decreased by one day.

➡

- We have cut emergency expenses by 3 percent so far, thanks to your prompt responses. Even better, we've had numerous e-mails from customers who appreciate our service.

> *Quick tip: Beware:* Many managers are hesitant about providing negative feedback, especially to lethargic employees whom they believe will be even less motivated if they are given negative feedback. Not so: Negative feedback can actually increase their motivation. Besides, the negative feedback is honest, and it shows that you're attuned to their performance. Just make sure you use a future-oriented voice and beware of negatives that leave the employees stranded in the past:
>
> *Negatives:* You did not reach your goal of 20 percent.
>
> *Future-oriented:* You reached 10 percent, but you still need to reach 20 percent.
>
> Here are more examples:
>
> - You still need to enter the information in the system by the first of the month—this month, you waited until the twentieth.
> - You need to focus on completing the forms every Friday. You were much better about that this week, but you still missed a few deadlines, which backed up the pay schedule for some employees.
> - Be sure to follow up immediately. You're still waiting up to a week to do so.

Create a Sense of Purpose and of Contributing to a Mission

Often, managers simply assign tasks, put together teams, and hand out responsibilities, as if they existed in a vacuum. Yet every job has a purpose—or should—which is to contribute to the company's mission. So draw a connection between the two when assigning tasks and giving feedback. Notice the difference:

Task oriented: Your job is to get approvals from our 20 most critical partners by Friday.

Mission oriented: The project will be successful only if you get approvals from our 20 most critical partners by Friday.

Task oriented: You need to sell protection plans with our cars.

Mission oriented: We want to make sure our customers aren't left stranded should they be in an accident with our protection plan.

Task oriented: Get the information in on time.

Mission oriented: Make sure our client has critical data on time.

Create a Sense of Belonging to a Group

Connecting an employee's duties, behaviors, and work approach to the well-being of the group can be a powerful motivating force. Here are some ways to achieve this:

- Once you compile the test results, Jeb and I will develop the presentation.

- As part of the team, you will be responsible for …
- So your team can make this deadline, you will …
- As an expert in … you'll play a critical role in helping the client support team.
- Be prepared to help the team by … This will be critical to our success.
- To get this project off the ground, we need you to …
- Our goal is to … You need to … or we won't reach it.

> *Quick tip:* Assign tasks in meetings when the entire team is present—and follow up on these tasks in subsequent meetings.

> *Yet another quick tip:* Don't confuse a happy employee with a motivated one: A social butterfly may enjoy flittering from office to office for a chat. Motivated? Not really. In fact, the employee *could* be depleting the motivation—and productivity—of coworkers. Instead, your employee needs to be task oriented and assume ownership of his or her success.

How to Handle Unmotivated Employees in Meetings

When You Have to Assign Tasks to Your Team

You need to compel unmotivated employees to participate fully and enthusiastically. Be specific so that they can take full responsibility for the success or failure of their tasks:

- This is the most important report we produce all year. You need to interact with the other components to make sure we get accurate information from them.

- If we lapse in getting our budget in on time, we may lose the funding. So you need to get the right figures and send the budget request on time, if not earlier.
- You and Paige should touch base every morning to support each other and remain on task.
- Since you have experience with these matters, please lay out guidelines that take us through the first six months.

When You Have a Problem or Perplexing Issue

Unmotivated employees need to get involved too. It's helpful to address these employees in a group to give them a sense of involvement and responsibility. Have them follow up in some visible way, such as with e-mails or presentations:

- Write down three or four ways of managing this problem and e-mail everyone by Friday.
- I know you've addressed situations like this before. Please prepare a page or so detailing the lessons you've learned and how we can apply them. Then post it on our portal.
- What do you think is the best way to address this issue? Please prepare a brief plan for next week's meeting.
- Since this is within your area of expertise, please evaluate our next steps and help us determine how we can improve.
- Please outline the best outcome we can hope for and the most critical steps we must take to achieve it. Then be prepared to discuss it at the team meeting next week.
- Take a look at the plan and e-mail your responses. We'll incorporate your thoughts as we move forward.

When the Team Seems Unmotivated

- We're the only ones with the expertise in this area to make this project a success.

- No question, we can make this project work, and the client depends on us. What are some ways we can fulfill this mission?
- Let's review our goals for this project, and we'll check back next month at this time to see how well we've reached them.
- Our goal is to complete the report in 25 percent less time than last year. To meet that goal, we need to reduce the time we spend responding to the client's questions from answering about two questions a week to answering two a day.

How to Handle Unmotivated Employees in One-on-One Situations

When You're Hoping to Get Them to Participate More Fully Than Before

- Here's the situation we have to address. How do you think you can help us?
- We need someone who's really strong in ... Can you help us?
- Which teams do you think can best use your area of expertise?
- We can fulfill our goal of launching this project on time if you take on the following new responsibilities: ...
- Last year, you were engaged in Phases 1 and 2, but this year we need your expertise for all four phases.

When They Have Great Potential and You Need to Tap Into It

- This project must be a priority for you: Your contribution is indispensable to our making the June 5 deadline.

- Your past director says you're really strong in this area. We'd like you to contribute in these ways: …
- I want you to take responsibility for … I think you're the best person to do it.
- Last year, you helped the team complete the project on time and within budget even though we were short three employees. We need that kind of help again this year.

Passive-Aggressive Employees

Passive-aggressive employees present serious challenges to any manager. These employees communicate indirectly, and they are frequently disingenuous. They commit to responsibilities, and then they find surreptitious ways to avoid them. And they complain—but rarely constructively. In meetings, the passive–aggressive types may support your analysis of a situation and agree to be responsible for follow-up actions. But afterward, they may sabotage you on many fronts—degrading your ideas or misplacing important materials you need right away. They frequently show up late, miss deadlines, and encounter an impressive array of problems, from an inordinate number of hard-drive crashes to e-mailed messages that mysteriously vanish in cyberspace … again.

So you must be especially diligent when communicating with these employees. Here's what you do.

Document Every Assignment

Be especially diligent and specific because your passive-aggressive employees will be quick to blame you for not giving clear direction:

- You must call at least 35 companies on our list each morning between 9:00 and 12:00. In the afternoon, you should document these calls, in detail, and then follow up with them through an e-mail or faxed letter.

- By May 12, you should have completed the preliminary steps of this project and be prepared to move on to the implementation phase.

- If you have trouble, please contact Jules at extension 1357. Otherwise, I expect to receive the completed report on my desk by noon, as we discussed last week.
- You will work with Aaron and Sean on the tasks we outlined in our meeting, and you should reach each of your personal deadlines on time or early.
- Every time you receive a customer comment, describe it on this form and get it to me by the end of the day.

Follow Up with an E-Mail

And make sure you get your employees to agree to your terms:

- Let me know if you have any ideas or questions. If I don't hear from you, I'll assume you are clear about your responsibilities.
- Please confirm that these are the steps we agreed on this afternoon.
- Please sign the attached agreement and leave it on my desk so that we can be clear about tasks and deadlines.

Follow Up in Writing After Every Major Conversation— and Even After Some Minor Ones

Use E-Mail to Restate a Point

- As we discussed in our meeting on Friday, …
- I've written each of the steps we agreed to on Monday. If problems interfere with your progress, let me know immediately and we'll find solutions.
- Here are the steps you recommended on Friday. If you need to make changes, let me know.
- I've reviewed your changes to the agreement—it looks good to me. I look forward to seeing … results.

- It's important that you stick to the plans we outlined Friday so that we can avoid the confusion we experienced during the last project.

Provide Constant Follow-Up

- Please let me know the status of this project.
- By now you should be doing … Are you on target? Please e-mail me and let me know.
- As we agreed, you should be tracking your efforts. Could you send me your status at this point?
- Please answer the following questions so that I can be clear about your status.
- I would like to meet with you at noon to discuss your progress so far.
- As we agreed last week, you were to accomplish … I assume you are about to finish this task. Where do you plan to go from here?

> *Quick tip:* Since they see themselves as victims, passive-aggressive employees are usually the first ones to launch a lawsuit. So keep track of every meeting and save every agreement. These documents may prove handy later.

Assign Ownership of the Problem

Make sure your passive-aggressive employees take ownership of their problems—and the solutions to them. Remember, passive-aggressive employees are experts at concocting problems that interfere with their progress:

- You were late in meeting your deadline twice last week. Please write the reasons why and how you can overcome these problems in the future.
- Since you have had numerous computer problems, you need to set up a reliable back-up procedure so that you can continue working if hard drive problems arise. For example, you can use the unoccupied office and computer, or you can bring your laptop to work as a back-up. Please give me a brief contingency plan with your status report by close of day.
- Please write down all the problems that interfered with your completing the … Then write a solution for each so that you won't face these problems again.
- Since you have had trouble reaching Carmela, I asked her to send you alternative numbers where she can be reached. E-mail me so that I know you received them.
- I am sending along the project plan. You need to indicate any areas that have given you trouble in the past—and alternatives to them. Then I expect you to make every deadline and provide all the information necessary.
- How do you think we could do it better?
- What do you think you could have done to improve that situation?
- Let's meet again and see how we can address those problems.
- Everyone has experienced those situations, and it's out of our team's control. Here's how we can work around it.
- I'm glad you approached me about these problems, and I'll be watching out for them. If they interfere with your progress again, let me know, and we'll find ways you can still keep on track.

Describe Other Behavior Problems

Use the most objective terms possible and outline the behavior you want. Show the connection between the employee's behavior problem and a work-related outcome:

Subjective: You were rude in the office yesterday and upset many of your colleagues.

Objective: You swore at Gina twice yesterday in front of Dana and Martha. You must stop using expletives in the office or when conducting our business anywhere.

- You need to stick to the deadlines. Last month you missed three out of seven of them by several weeks, and this held up our reports.
- You must keep your voice low, especially in the office. Several people with desks at the far end of the hall have complained that the noise is distracting to customers.
- Be sure to come to the meetings prepared. We had to delay the last two staff meetings while you searched for documents.
- You arrived at work after 10:00 a.m. three times last week. The day begins at 8:30, as you know. Be sure to arrive on time and ready for meetings.

When Necessary, Cite Portions of Your Employee Manual or Some Other Source

- According to the employee manual, you must never …
- Company policy indicates that you can never … regardless of the circumstances.

- According to federal regulations, an employee in your position should never ...
- According to company policy, you cannot ... under any conditions.
- As you can see from our communications guidelines, the proper steps are to ...
- Never discuss those issues with customers. This is clearly stated in our customer service manual.

> *Quick tip:* Be prepared to point the employee to that document—and the specific page. Where necessary, quote excerpts in your communication.

Approach Them as Team Members

Like unmotivated employees, the passive-aggressives must be encouraged to feel a part of the group—but for a different reason. Passive-aggressive employees will try to feel singled out and present themselves as victims. That strategy becomes harder if everyone is expected to share similar goals and responsibilities:

- You'll be part of Fred's group—your mission is to complete ...
- Our goal, as a unit, is to ... That means all of you should ...
- You need to reach this deadline by January 16. So everyone needs to provide ...
- To reach our target, all of you must ...
- I expect the entire team to expedite this process within three days.

Use These Other Phrases Too

When Developing Goals, Responsibilities, and Agreements

- Here are the steps we agreed on. Do you have any comments or changes you think we should make?
- Here are the assignments you and I agreed you would complete this month.
- What are your goals for each assignment this quarter? Please be specific because we'll review them later.
- I have listed each of your responsibilities for this assignment. Are there any issues that will get in the way of your reaching them? If so, let me know by tomorrow afternoon so that we can address them.
- These are the four goals we agreed you must reach by the end of the month. E-mail me by the end of the week if you want to modify them.

When Shifting Responsibilities or Adding to Them

- Everyone on our team needs to change direction because of the director's new mandate. So you now need to …
- You did great work on the *A* project. For now, though, put it on hold because our team needs to focus on *B*. Afterward, you can return to *A*.
- You need to accomplish *X* before the first of the month. Let's determine some ways you can do that while keeping on track with the other assignments.
- We just learned that our client needs *Y* by next week. We need your help in getting it to her. Let me know what tasks you can put on hold until next week.

■ Please e-mail your ideas about the best way to make the *X, Y,* and *Z* deadlines on time.

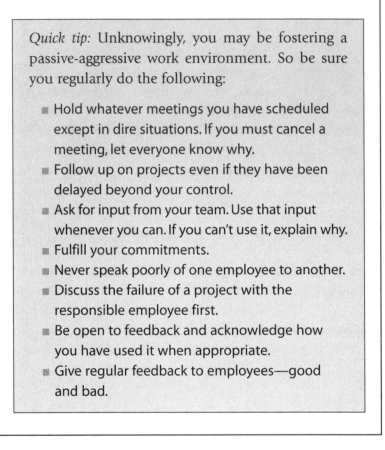

Quick tip: Unknowingly, you may be fostering a passive-aggressive work environment. So be sure you regularly do the following:

■ Hold whatever meetings you have scheduled except in dire situations. If you must cancel a meeting, let everyone know why.

■ Follow up on projects even if they have been delayed beyond your control.

■ Ask for input from your team. Use that input whenever you can. If you can't use it, explain why.

■ Fulfill your commitments.

■ Never speak poorly of one employee to another.

■ Discuss the failure of a project with the responsible employee first.

■ Be open to feedback and acknowledge how you have used it when appropriate.

■ Give regular feedback to employees—good and bad.

Angry Employees

Anger ranks among the most toxic feelings a manager can confront. In fact, only one thing is worse than confronting an angry employee, and that's *not* confronting the employee. In these cases, employees act out their emotions indirectly: talking behind your back, sabotaging projects by missing deadlines, and giving less than 100 percent. So make sure you provide an environment in which employees can speak to you openly and honestly—without negating your control! Here are some phrases that can help.

Show That You Notice Their Anger

Stay alert for signs that employees might be angry—especially when work pressure gets higher than usual. Ask them how they are feeling—without assuming anything:

- Do you have anything you want to speak with me about?
- Are you okay?
- How are things going with the project?
- If you confront any obstacles or want to discuss anything with me, I'll be in my office all day.
- Is anything going on that I should know about?
- I'd like an update about the project—what are your impressions so far?
- Anything you need to tell me about how you're feeling about work?
- I'm interested in your thoughts, so please tell me.

Focus On Feelings First

Anger, as you surely know, ranks as one of the most consuming emotions we experience. It can block out employees' reasoning ability and also their ability to listen and understand. So you must first address the emotional states of these employees—not necessarily by calling attention to them but by calming the employees down. Then get them to express the causes of their anger:

- You need to relax a minute.
- Calm down and then tell me what you're thinking.
- Take a few breaths and then we'll talk.
- Do you want to get some water?
- Are you okay? Want a few minutes?

Don't Let Your Employees Wallow in Anger

The feeling will only build or, equally bad, fester. Instead, address the anger immediately:

- Why don't you sit down and tell me what you're thinking.
- Let's look at your concerns and see how we can address them.
- Tell me specifically what's bothering you.
- I know you have strong feelings, and I'd like to hear them.
- What, exactly, are you thinking?
- I'm surprised to see you're so angry—what's the problem?
- I'd like to address your feeling about this.

> *Quick tip: The 10-Minute Rule:* Wait 10 minutes, but not much longer, before confronting employees who have had outbursts so that they can calm down and respond rationally—not emotionally. Then respond confidently and quickly to ensure that you have control.

Let Your Employees Cool Down

In some cases, you may need to delay your meeting with angry employees because of schedule issues and other matters. In that case, you might say:

- I want to know more about what you're thinking. Why not come to my office at 3:00 so that we can talk?
- This really deserves some focus. E-mail me about when we can meet, either this afternoon or tomorrow morning.
- We need to address this issue privately, so let's meet in my office on Thursday. How does 11:00 sound?
- Why don't you write a list of the core issues we should address and then meet with me tomorrow afternoon to discuss them.

Quick tip: Some employees are more than willing to vent in a meeting—even about peripheral issues. Have an audience? All the better. In this case, you need to tell them that to avoid spreading their negative feelings to the rest of your team and derailing the agenda, you'll address their concerns later. Make sure you're clear about when you plan to talk so that other employees know you fully intend to address the issue. In the process, you'll promote an atmosphere of openness.

Use Some of These Phrases to Handle Employees Who Express Anger During Meetings

If employees reveal anger in meetings, use this two-part strategy:

Acknowledge   Plan

- (*acknowledge*) Since your feelings are so strong, (*plan*) we should talk about them separately. Let's meet in my office first thing Monday for about an hour.
- (*acknowledge*) I think we should discuss this separately. (*plan*) Schedule a meeting with me later.
- (*acknowledge*) Why don't you write these thoughts down, (*plan*) and then schedule a meeting to discuss them with me?
- (*acknowledge*) You already mentioned that point. (*plan*) I'd like you to come up with some solutions and discuss them with me—in my office—later tomorrow.
- (*acknowledge*) Why don't you hold those feelings for now, and we'll spend time talking about them later. (*plan*) Talk to me after this meeting to find a time.

If angry employees vent later in the meetings, refer to your most recent conversation:

- As I said, we should talk about this later.
- Once you write down those thoughts, we'll discuss them systematically.
- Save this for our one-on-one meeting also.
- We'll review this point later.
- As I said, we need to let other people take the floor. We'll talk separately.
- Put this on our agenda for that meeting.
- This will have to wait—as I said.

Discuss what's appropriate. Let your out-of-control employees know the appropriate means available to them for expressing anger:

➡

- If you have issues you want to address, you must be rational and systematic in your approach. Name-calling and raising your voice won't help and are against company policy.

- You need to find the right times to express your views. In front of customers is not one of them.

- You need to raise your concerns with me privately, in my office or by e-mail. At meetings, we need to stay on track, and we can't digress to spend time on issues that concern only you.

- You need to determine precisely what the problem is and the solutions you think would help. Outbursts will help none of us.

- Please reserve your viewpoints for appropriate times and places. The communications guideline will help.

Beware the "Anger" Trap

Don't attempt to label angry feelings as such. To you, it looks like anger. And, indeed, it may be anger. But defensive, passive-aggressive, or overly sensitive employees may hide behind words. Ask such employees to explain their anger and they might derail any discussion by saying "I'm not angry" or by relegating such feelings to less intense words such as *frustrated* or *upset*. Instead, say:

- I'd like to know how you're feeling.
- You seem to have some strong feelings about this matter.
- Since you have a great deal to say about office policies, I thought we should talk.
- I'm interested in what you're thinking.
- I know you have a lot of thoughts about this matter—I'd like to know more.

Ask for Clarification

- What did you mean by that last point?
- I wasn't clear about what you meant when you said "unfair." Do you mean to the customer? Or to the employees?
- Can you repeat that last statement—just so I get it right?
- Did you or the customer say that?
- Did anyone see the interaction?
- How many times do you think you were in this position?

Create Synergy and Understanding

When possible, build a sense of synergy and understanding. For example, you may fully accept the reasons for the anger some employees feel: Perhaps another unit interfered with their progress needlessly, or perhaps circumstances didn't go their way. So it's important to validate your employees' feelings—without suggesting this entitles them to destructive rage.

Try to Show Support Whether or Not You Agree

- I can see how you feel that way.
- That's an interesting point of view, and we should pay attention to it.

- I'm sure other people feel that way as well. Now here's what really happened.
- I had no idea that's how you saw the situation.
- That's a tough outlook—I see why your feelings are so strong.
- That's how I felt too.

Try to Show Support Even If You Don't Understand What Is Being Said

It may be difficult or impossible to understand employees who are speaking too quickly, making too many points at once, or contradicting themselves. When that's the case, use these expressions:

- Let me summarize what you just said, and tell me if I have it right.
- What I think you said was this: …
- Am I right in thinking you made these major points: …
- Just to clarify, did you mean that …
- I want to understand what you're saying, so please repeat that last point slowly so I can get it.

Once Your Employees Have Stated Their Position, State Yours

Be entirely objective, relying on specific incidents and outcomes to support your point. Beware of discussing your emotional reactions:

- As I recall, the situation occurred this way: …
- I understand your point; however, the policy manual requires that I …
- He has a stellar record, in fact, more customers compliment him than any other employee.

- Your job description specifically states that you need to be responsible for those matters.
- If you look on the project plan, you'll see that you need to …
- To get a promotion, you need to have … as you will see in the job description posted online.

Come to an Agreement

Keep your discussion forward looking. Sure, something negative happened, but focus on ways you can get through those difficulties or on lessons you can learn in the future. Make your comments action oriented so that you and your angry employees can take definite and identifiable steps to avert volatile situations in the future. And, above all, make sure the employees agree to all the steps—out loud. And take notes—you might need them later.

- So here are the three main ways we can avoid this in the future.
- I will get back to you about this within two days.
- We agreed that you will do the following: …
- These are the steps you said you'd take next. Let me know if I can help.
- So we agree on the following points: …
- What I'm taking away from all this is … Do you agree?
- So we agree on these points … let me know if you have anything to add.
- This is where we'll go from here … Does that sound good?
- I'll see what I can do, and if you come up with ideas, let me know.

➡

When Possible, Try to Get Employees to Provide Actionable Feedback

This will help employees have ownership of the follow-up action—and the results:

- How could this situation have gone better?
- What are some specific ways we could improve the office in this regard?
- What are the three or four changes you would like to make?
- List the three most important steps you think our team could take to improve this situation.
- Give me some examples of how others have successfully addressed situations like this one.
- Let's make a quick list of all the things that you feel strongly about, and then go back and look for ways to resolve them.

When Possible, Follow Up with an Action Plan

- Over the next two weeks, you're going to …
- I want you to document … and then get back to me in two weeks. We'll see how the situation has improved.
- I'm going to reassign you to … Let me know how that works.
- I'm going to talk to Carol and see what we can do. Then she'll get back to you—by early January at the latest.

> *Quick tip:* Have angry or volatile employees? Don't know how to deal with them? Think they may be suffering from mental health issues that are at the heart of the problem! Then contact HR immediately.

Stuck-in-the-Box Performers

Employees can get stuck in old and frequently unimpressive patterns for a range of reasons. The most obvious: They're simply *not* out-of-the-box thinkers. They seize one way of doing things and cling to it—no matter *what*. Deadlines and pressures also rank among the top factors pounding employees into stuck-in-the-box submission. Who has time to think up new approaches when the deadline clock is ticking … and 10 other deadlines are waiting in line right after that? So employees click into autopilot, the fastest way to get things done, and then they move to the next project. Besides, who can focus on creative solutions when his or her attention gets splintered by ever-changing requirements, unexpected demands, and impatient clients or colleagues wanting a dozen things all at once?

Just as critical, employees are plagued by a litany of fears that function like psychological cement shoes: fear of failure, fear of risk, fear of ridicule, fear of the spotlight. They simply drown in them. How much easier to work on predictable projects with predictable outcomes: What a relief.

Still, you can get creative solutions from the most stuck-in-the-box performers. How do you bring them out? What perfect phrases will activate the latent creativity in all of them? This section will explain.

Set Aside Time in Staff Meetings for New Ideas

Try to make meetings be problem specific. The more difficult the problem, the more time you should spend discussing solution:

- What are some ideas for letting customers know about the changes?
- What kinds of messages will best help us reach …
- We can position this many ways. I'd like to hear some ideas.
- Last year we … This year we need something fresher— more exciting. What do you think?
- We need some ideas for the annual conference, and the theme needs to tie into the annual report. What are some ideas?

> *Quick tip:* Partner employees with complementary skills, or create work groups of two or three employees to find inspired ideas and present them to the group.

When Possible, Create a Framework for Conversation

Not general requests: What's a better way to approach this?

But specific ones: Think up two ways of approaching this—one at each end of the spectrum of possibility. Take them as far as you can. Later we'll find solutions in the middle.

Not general requests: How can we fix this problem?

But specific ones: What are three possible ways of fixing this problem? Be creative. Think up something entirely new.

Not general requests: We need to find ways of getting through these blocks.

But specific ones: Here are the four biggest blocks we have to get through to make this project work. See if you can come up with one or two solutions for each of them, and present your ideas on Friday. I don't care how goofy or outrageous, by the way. Go to town.

Work Off of Successful Ideas from Other Projects

See how you can adapt or build on them:

- If you remember, last year we … How can we increase by 10 percent?
- Tom's idea was to … He had great results. How can we get that to work for us?
- The Foster model indicates that we should take five steps. How do you think we can cut it down to three?
- The other team found that … was helpful. But I think we can do even better, don't you?

Avoid Questions That Will Get Yes or No Answers

They're definitely conversation stoppers:

Conversation stopper: Does anyone have any ideas about ways to apply the formula?

Conversation opener: What are two, maybe three ways, we can apply the formula?

Conversation stopper: Can anyone determine a better way to do this?

Conversation opener: What are three better ways to do this?

Encourage Free-Flowing Conversation

Remain open to any ideas, no matter how outrageous. Instead, consider them fodder for better things to come.

In a Meeting

- That's an interesting idea. Let's take it to the next level.
- Let's put that one in the parking lot and get back to it.
- Does anyone want to add to that idea?
- How would you apply that idea to the most common scenario?
- Does anyone want to add to that idea and see what we get?

In a One-on-One Discussion

- Great. What are a few other ideas you can think of?
- Can you show me how you'd apply that idea if … happened?
- Okay, let's write that down. Now what are two or three other possibilities?
- Yes, and if we work off of that idea, here's what we can get: …
- Let's make two changes to that idea and see where it takes us.
- That idea would work really well with a … How can we adapt it to our current situation?

> *Quick tip:* In a meeting, write all new ideas on a flip chart or white board. Then return to those ideas later. Resist the temptation to shake your head no at an idea or, worse, insult it.

➡

Add Spice

Perk up your employees by tapping into their competitive spirit or their desire for awards. Here are some ways to do that and set some really cool goals with even cooler rewards at the end.

Tap the Competitive Spirit

- What are some ways we can do a better job than …
- We already know what our competitors are up to. Let's figure out the secret to their success—then find ways to do it better.
- Let's dust them—how are we going to do it?
- They've been the leading … long enough. Let's find ways to wipe them off the map.
- How are we going to win the … account? It's got to be innovative, and it has to excite them. Ideas, please.
- The competitor won that account three years in a row, and it cost us millions. Now let's figure out ways to win it back.

Tap the Goal-Oriented Soul

- Right now, we're number 8. Not bad out of 100, but not good enough. How are we going to get there?
- Let's go for 25 percent over last year. I know it sounds ambitious, and it is. What are we going to do to get there?
- For five years we've been getting 15 percent of the market. Let's think up some really strong new strategies that will win us 25 percent.
- When you started here, we were … We can get a lot better, but the old ways won't get us there. Come up with some ideas and let's talk about it.

➡

Tap the Award-Loving Individual

- Let's find some innovative strategies that will win us the Excellence Award.
- Right now, we're rated at *B*-plus. So what do we have to do to get that up to an *A*?
- If we're really innovative, we'll make our goals and get that bonus.
- This year I want to see our team getting the award. So how are we going to do it?

Quick tip: Share unusual, and successful, ideas from other professionals. Discuss them for 5 or 10 minutes in your weekly meeting; e-mail interesting articles or ideas; point out inspiring television programs on PBS or the Discovery Channel. Encourage other employees to discuss them at strategy sessions or host brown-bag lunches. These efforts will get your team thinking creatively and will inspire stuck-in-the-box performers as well.

Immediately Follow Up on Ideas You Plan to Use

Be specific and give credit where credit is due:

- As you suggested in the meeting, we'll start …
- Take a look at the enclosed marketing piece. It reflects the innovation and imagination from the brainstorming session.
- From now on, we're going to implement the process we discussed …

- The new approach that Frank developed has already brought rewards.
- Thanks, Stacey, for your great idea. We plan to begin implementing it next week.
- We predict the new model that the accounting team developed will save us …
- The customers have been raving about …
- We received the attached e-mails from customers saying how much they appreciate …

> *Quick tip:* Sometimes employees need fresh blood, new insights, and unusual ideas. So bring in someone from the outside—whether a colleague or a seasoned creativity trainer. Make sure this person discusses the risks other professionals took with their innovative approaches. You may not have time for full-day creativity training, but brown-bag lunches, a half-day session, or even an hour talk at a staff meeting can work wonders.

How to Settle Disputes Between Employees

Conflicts between employees are inevitable—and not necessarily bad. In fact, most conflict resolution experts agree that a healthy workforce is a dynamic one in which employees can openly discuss differing opinions and approaches. So the best thing you can do is to foster *healthy* communication among employees by being forthright with information, finding time for employees to discuss core issues as a team, and rewarding their input with praise.

Trouble can begin when employees attack each other's personal attributes, speak of one another in pejorative terms, or categorically condemn each other as bad employees or, even, people. The discussion is no longer professional or productive but negative, and it can create serious divides. How you address the problems depends on the employees' personalities, work styles, and work histories. In most cases, though, you can resolve the struggle through the strategies in this section.

Invite the Employees to a Meeting Using Neutral Language

Charged language: We have to end this battle right away.

Neutral language: We need to find equilibrium.

Charged language: You have to stop being bitter enemies.

Neutral language: You need to have a strong working relationship.

Charged language: We have no room for hate or personal animosity.

Neutral language: We must show respect for each other all the time.

Here are a few more examples:

- We need to resolve this situation immediately.
- I want to discuss ways we can move forward.
- I want both of you to contribute to our team in the most productive and positive manner possible.
- This will be an opportunity for you to talk constructively.
- We will take this time to determine a productive path moving forward.
- We need to determine goals and ways you can work together to reach them.

Quick tip: By holding one meeting with both employees involved in the argument, you will dispel the opinion that you're partial to one of them.

Establish Ground Rules for the Discussion

- You cannot call each other names either in this office or any other time while engaged in company business.
- I want you to focus on what happened, not on your feelings about what happened.
- You must support any point, concern, or suggestion with a concrete example.
- I don't want to hear anything hypothetical. Every thought, idea, or suggestion must be based in reality. Please provide names, dates, and even locations unless other people are involved and you need to maintain their confidentiality.

- I don't want to hear what anyone else said, any rumors, gossip, or outside opinions. If you need to pull in third-party opinions, make sure you have it in writing and it refers to circumstances, not personal tastes.

- We're going to discuss where we are today and where we hope to be, moving forward. Let's not dredge up old issues that are irrelevant to our meeting today.

> *Quick tip:* Be sure to apply each of these rules throughout the discussion—and be diligent. An employee may not call another employee "stupid," but saying a process the employee implemented was "stupid" is about the same.

Here are more phrases for laying out ground rules:

- We need to approach this as productively as we can.

- When we finish this discussion, we need to develop a game plan. So make sure you give examples of what you think the problem is and immediately follow with solutions.

- We're all working for the same goals, so let's figure out a way to get there.

- You need to follow these guidelines so that we get the best outcome from this discussion.

- Each of you will have a chance to speak—but I'll let you know when.

- Keep focused on events—not attitudes.

Take a Future-Oriented Perspective with This Two-Step Approach

Step 1. Get the Employees to Outline the Situation They Want to Remedy

Objective language is critical. Notice the difference:

Subjective: Ronnie isn't a team player …

Objective: Ronnie keeps e-mailing the customer about changes without telling us, so we lose track of the project. Several times we have missed deadlines because of this.

Subjective: Yes, I am a team player.

Objective: I told them about the changes—they just forgot.

Step 2. Address Strategies for Solving the Problem in the Future

Keep it actionable and specific:

General: Ronnie should keep everyone updated about his conversations with the customer.

Specific: Ronnie should copy Rita and Howard when he e-mails the customer so he or she will be clear about changes in plans.

When addressing numerous disagreements between employees, try not to clump the issues together:

- Okay, let's look at these issues one at a time.
- What do you think is the most important issue we need to address?

- We only have one hour, so let's focus on the two or three most important matters we need to resolve.
- I want to discuss that incident between you last week, and then I want to discuss the role each of you played in compiling that proposal.
- I noticed several work habits that I want both of you to change when you work together. I'm going to start with the most obvious.

Use Nonjudgmental Language Throughout

You can do this by acknowledging the content of the communication—without judging it:

Judgmental: We heard Mike's perspective. Do you disagree with anything he said?

Nonjudgmental: Do you want to discuss any of these points?

Nonjudgmental: Do you have anything to add?

Nonjudgmental: Do you have anything else to say on the subject?

Judgmental: Do you want to discuss why you're angry?

Nonjudgmental: Do you want to discuss any workplace issues?

Judgmental: Are you frustrated with this project?

Nonjudgmental: How do you feel about this project?

Judgmental: So what went wrong last week?

Nonjudgmental: So what happened last week?

Avert Personal Accusation

- You need to stick to facts throughout this discussion.
- You need to give me an example of when that occurred to clarify what you mean.
- Back up and tell me what happened from a process point of view and what you believe should have happened.
- I want both of you to tell me two or three ways you fostered the situation.
- How did that affect our processes here?

Avoid Getting Stuck in the Problem

- What do you think we can do about that—as a team?
- What steps did you take, and which ones should you have taken instead?
- I think I understand what happened. How can we avoid this in the future?
- How did you avoid these types of problems in the past?
- I'd like each of you to mention three or four things that you could have done differently.
- What would you like to have Tom do so that you can have a better working relationship?

Let the Situation End on a Positive Note

- I think we covered a lot here today. I look forward to seeing how well you work together.
- I want you to think about quick and effective ways you can address problems in the future.
- I think the issues are pretty straightforward and we can move on, don't you agree?
- At this point, you should have no problem getting along. I look forward to the improvement.

- You did a great job of communicating—this bodes well for the future.
- I think the issues are pretty clear and that you will do well to put them behind you.

If Meeting Separately with Employees, Make Sure You Continue Using Neutral Language

Get Each Person's Opinion

- What is your take on the situation?
- What do you think are the core issues we must address?
- How did that problem start in the first place?
- What was your role in the dynamic?
- At what stage do you think things started to change?

Discuss How Each Employee Can Help Remedy the Situation

- What do you think you could have done differently?
- How can we resolve that problem moving forward?
- What are some of the internal supports that can help address that problem?
- What organizational factors do you think contributed to this dynamic?
- Have you learned anything from this situation?
- What do you see as a positive vision for the future?

> *Quick tip:* The meeting should occur in a neutral area—your office, perhaps—and should be confidential. If you have an assistant who takes notes at your meetings, now is not the best time to invite that person.

How to Motivate Employees Who Resist Change

Change is the only constant in just about any workplace. Employees can perceive change in one of two ways, depending on how you present it. It can excite, energize, and offer numerous opportunities, or it can mean that employees lose control, that they must veer from a familiar and comfortable path, and that they have to exert energy on new and seemingly difficult tasks. The difference in their choice between these responses can depend on how you communicate that change and what employees see as opportunities for success.

Set the Right Tone from the Beginning

- We're going to be targeting a new set of objectives.
- Our CEO introduced changes that will help the company reach critical financial goals, including …
- We're going to participate in a new initiative at the company. It should be challenging, but it can yield great rewards.
- We're going to be reorienting some projects and adding new ones as part of greater initiative to …

Use Strong, Forward-Looking Verbs When Possible

Don't Use These Terms

- Undergo
- Subject to
- Fall under (the mandate …)
- Under (these changes)

Do Use These Terms

- Launch
- Target
- Participate
- Move forward

Be Open to Discussion When Addressing Initial Push-Back

- Let's look at your core concerns and address the details later.
- We're going to draft a plan next week to implement these changes. Then, by Thursday at the latest, we'll hold a meeting to further discuss how we'll make this work.
- We'll have regular meetings to solve problems as we go.
- As you can see, we've established clear goals, and we will continue finding better ways to reach them.
- This is the direction the company is taking. As you'll see in upcoming weeks, you'll get plenty of information and support from the corporate office and from me.

Indicate how, specifically and quantitatively, the employees will help support the change:

- What will the changes look like?
- How will life differ from the way it was?
- What can employees expect?
- What will they experience?

➡

Give Specific Information So That Employees Have a Sense of Control

Here are sample phrases you can use:

- You will be assigned to separate teams of five people each, and the teams will be reassigned to specific regional territories in the Southwest.
- Over the next few weeks, about half of you will be reassigned to another district. If you choose not to go, then you have the option of …
- Currently, you are responsible for … Moving forward, you will be responsible for …
- In our old business model, we expected that you would bring these results: … Now though, you need to bring these results: … This may seem like a huge difference, but actually it isn't.
- The leadership will be divided into three new groups, each with its own units. You will be in this unit: …
- We will operate in smaller but more technologically advanced research centers. For example, instead of … we will have … This will give us many advantages, such as …

Be Honest

Let employees know about some of the frustrations and slowdowns you expect, and tell them you predict that these will be short-lived:

- This is how the process will look: …
- At first, our systems will take a few minutes longer, but that should only last …

- You will have a learning curve, no question, but you'll receive world-class training to help you incorporate the new information as quickly as possible.
- Some of you will need to relocate: …
- By 2010, here's what you can expect: …

Establish Goals So That Employees Can Recognize When They're Succeeding

This will help them overcome a sense of futility or hunger for the past. Be sure to use the present as a starting point and include the benefits of the move, when possible. This is how your structure should look:

Now   Later   Benefits

For example:

> (*now*) We'll stop wasting 20 percent of our budget on travel, (*later*) which will free up your time (*benefits*) by hours or more every day.

> Here are a few more perfect phrases using this formula:

- We currently have a strong presence in only two of five territories. By making these changes, we'll have a presence in at least four and potentially increase our profit margin by …
- The office cannot accommodate our growing employee base, so we need to move to a larger facility that will accommodate everyone.
- We are not keeping up with our competitors in terms of how we use technology, so everyone will go through the training module. In the long run, this will

If the benefit happens to be impressive—or surprising in a positive sense—then mention it first in your sentence:

- We can potentially increase our market share by 50 percent if we move from a system of … to one in which …
- We can tap into a highly professional employee base and successfully double our size by moving from our current location to this university town.
- You will have access to more of the tools you want because money will be freed up by cutting back on … and …

Get Employees to Identify Obstacles to the Change

These could include things like insufficient support, outdated tools, or inadequate training:

Don't use negative or "blocking" language: What are some problems that you think will get in your way?

Use positive language: What do you think will help you move forward?

Don't use negative or blocking language: What is going to be most difficult problem you confront?

Use positive language: How can the company best support you?

Here are some more examples:

- What kinds of training will help you adjust the fastest? We have Web and in-class training.
- What do you think will be most helpful for your team?
- What is the smoothest way to get through this transition?

➡

- The opportunities include …
- This transition does offer numerous opportunities.

Lead—Don't Force

One reason employees resist change is that they feel out of control. So, as a manager, the best thing you can do is to lead them through the change rather than force them to accept it. Otherwise, you may get a great deal of nodding heads when you announce the change and a great deal of resistance, negativity, and anger later. So how do you lead them? Here are a few strategies.

Use Future-Oriented Words

These include words such as *will* and avoid words like *must* when discussing changes:

Not: You must adjust to these changes.

But: You will adjust to these changes.

Not: You have to accept these changes.

But: You will accept these changes.

Not: You better get use to it.

But: You will get use to it.

Use *We* Whenever Possible

This helps to indicate that each employee is part of a team and working toward a common mission:

- Once we move, we will …
- Some of the new goals we will need to meet …

- Our new mission will be to … We can achieve this by …
- We will soon find that …

Provide Examples

Point to other times when organizations experienced similar changes and indicate how they succeeded:

- As you probably recall, during the technology bust in the late nineties, we went through similar changes. Yet today, our software division …
- We did need to downsize several years ago, but all of you retained your jobs and thrived, as you can see today.
- This cycle is predictable and necessary for the health of the company. For example, …
- We went through an identical situation in 1985. Within two years, we bounced back; in fact, our health was better than ever.
- Do you remember when … went through similar changes? Think about where they are today.
- According to business guru Tom Franklin, every growing organization goes through changes like these. In fact, it's what makes them strong. For example, …

> *Quick tip:* Use fewer, more powerful, messages. Otherwise, employees will get communications burnout and start skimming or otherwise ignoring your messages.

Adapt Messages from Your Corporate Office to Your Employees

Discuss How the Change Will Affect Their Jobs

- Most of the layoffs won't be affecting our area, although we will experience some.
- We'll go through the training process before the rest of the company because we're …
- The new name change will not affect us until February. At that point, you'll get new e-mail addresses …
- We plan to begin training in the spring, most likely. We're forth in line after … departments.
- We'll begin the move in about five years. Since we'll be the last to go, we'll probably be relocated nearby in the interim.

Highlight Opportunities or Supports Available to Them

- HR has opened an office with a full-time employee available to answer your questions about …
- The company will sponsor ongoing training to help you.
- We will bring in job placement specialists to help you identify other positions, write your résumé, and do well in interviews.
- I have a list of people you can call to answer your questions and provide you with other support as we move forward.
- You will find updates on our intranet site … You can also contact Valerie in HR at …
- The home office is compiling a list of places you can go for … I expect to receive the list by …

How to Address Push-Back without Slowing Progress

- So far, we've implemented changes like these successfully. So I expect the same to happen as we continue with the project plan.

- Why don't you find ways to address those issues and bring your solutions to the meeting next week? In the meantime, keep moving forward.

- Our goal was … So far, we have made progress, but we will need to address those issues at some point. Do you have any recommendations?

- Let's discuss these concerns in my office later today. The rest of you are invited too.

> *Quick tip:* Most people hear only about one of five words and they retain even fewer. So while you need to speak with employees and address their questions, make sure you combine other communications vehicles as well. Support your spoken message with a written reminder. Post lists on the intranet and provide them in hard copy. And provide charts, graphs, and other type of illustrations for more visually oriented employees.

Part Five

Perfect Phrases for Communicating with Difficult Customers

Unhappy customers can demonstrate their dissatisfaction in countless ways: public outbursts, telephone complaints, long letters documenting every conversation, or terse e-mails that copy the boss. And while you must focus on performance when communicating with coworkers and employees (if you're a manager), you need to focus on feelings when communicating with customers. Are they happy? Will they return? Because usually, the matter that enrages them may amount to as little as a few dollars or a few days they must spend waiting for a service or product. But their unhappiness, frustration, or anger will diminish their loyalty and spread to everyone they talk to about the matter. The resulting costs could be great.

Here are three things all customers want:

- *Customers want to be heard.* Granted, you may be "hearing" them through an e-mail, but the point is the same. Always listen closely—and let them know you're listening. If you're communicating in person, don't forget body language. Look them in the eye. Nod. Pause as you consider what they're saying. If you're writing to them, e-mail them right away and make plans for further discussions. And don't forget: Unhappy customers can tip you off to problems that no one—not you, your boss, or even customer surveys—has noticed.

- *Customers want to be loved.* You know the feeling. You pay for a service. You chose a product or service among many others. And you feel a loyalty to the brand you chose. So naturally, in return you want the company to be loyal to you. In fact, for many customers, the relationship is like a love affair. You need to remind them that you want them around, that you want to please them, and that, above all, they matter—even when they're angry, dissatisfied, or more generally impossible.

■ *Customers want something special.* The best way to soothe savage customers is give them something special. A comfortable place to sit while they wait longer than expected. A coupon for 20 percent off. Or a free cup of coffee. While these tokens of generosity may not cost much in dollars and cents, they're worth a lot, sometimes as much as a lifetime of devotion.

And yes—you can transform a troubled relationship with a difficult customer into a great business arrangement by applying a few simple strategies and some perfect phrases.

Angry Customers

The bad news is that angry customers can embarrass and insult you, even when you didn't cause their frustration. The good news is that most angry customers are easy to placate—and they may even turn into loyal (and more pleasant) customers later. Even better, strategies for soothing the savage customers don't entail whips, tranquilizers, or armed militias; perfect phrases will do.

Calm Outraged Customers, Focusing on Feelings First

- I see you're upset. Here, tell me the problem.
- Why don't you calm down, and we'll see how we can resolve this problem.
- Okay, relax, I'm here to help you.
- I didn't mean to get you upset. I'm sure we can resolve this.
- Sorry, I didn't mean to upset you. Here's what I meant.
- Why don't you relax a little, and we'll figure this out.

> *Quick tip:* Body language matters. Look at customers directly, without staring them down. Keep your body posture open and inviting. Nod your head. Smile. And remain focused.

Get Some Space

When customers make a scene in your lobby or office, separate them from the crowd. Talk them into going with you into a private setting by explaining the advantages of doing so:

- Why don't you come in my office where it's quiet and I can focus on what you're saying.

- Step over here, and I'll get you a glass of water.
- Have a seat in our waiting area. We can talk there, and you'll be more comfortable.
- Let's sit in our lounge. It's comfortable and we won't have any interruptions.
- Why don't we step outside so that you can have some privacy?
- Let's step over here where it's quieter and I can hear you better.

Avoid Using Leading Language in Written Communication to Customers

In letters or e-mails, calm customers in the first line. Avoid leading language:

Leading: I'm sorry you had to go through this. I'm sure it caused you great mental anguish.

Sympathetic: I'm sorry you had to go through this. I'm sure it wasn't pleasant.

Leading: Thank you for letting me know about that humiliating experience.

Sympathetic: I'm sorry to hear about that experience.

Thank Customers for Their Input When Responding to Complaints

- Thank you for letting me know about this situation.
- I appreciate your telling me your concerns.
- Thank you for giving me the chance to help you address this matter.

- Thank you for letting me know about the situation at the … branch.
- Thank you for telling me about your experience.
- I appreciate your taking the time to let me know about the situation at our store.

Assure Customers That You Can Help

- I am sure we can resolve this situation immediately.
- I appreciate the opportunity to clarify any misunderstandings.
- I'm sure I can explain what happened and find a good solution.
- I need to hear your point of view and then talk to our clerk about why it happened.
- Your input gives me an opportunity to resolve this problem.
- I know I can settle this easily.

Get to the Root of the Problem

Start by asking questions without making leading statements:

Leading: When did this terrible problem begin?

Neutral: Start from the beginning and tell me what happened.

Leading: How did he insult you?

Neutral: What did he say to you?

Leading: Which part of the bill did they get wrong?

Neutral: Which part of the bill concerns you?

Here are some other phrases:

- When exactly did this happen?
- Do you have any papers or e-mails that record this information?
- Can I see your contract—the specific wording will help me understand the situation.
- Can you tell me exactly what happened?
- What did you say afterward?

Sympathize

But don't blame your company or anyone in it:

Blame: I know that Anne can really be rude.

Sympathize: You should expect respect every time you walk in our doors.

Blame: The pricing isn't clear to anyone.

Sympathize: I can see you were confused.

Here are some other sympathetic phrases:

- I know that must have been difficult for you.
- The situation must have seemed perplexing.
- Yes, there are a lot of words on the policy statement.
- Web sites can be difficult to navigate.
- I'm sure the steps we took to reach that decision must seem complex.
- The industry language can seem confusing.

Don't Waste a Breath

Immediately after you sympathize, show how you can help:

- I can explain that to you.

- I believe I can help.
- Let me translate that into plain language.
- I can show you how.
- Let's walk through the … together.
- Why don't you ask me questions, and I'll help you understand.

Be There to Help

Show specifically how you will resolve problems if the customers' complaints are valid:

- The employee's manager will talk to him and ensure this situation doesn't recur.
- We will send you the refund immediately by overnight mail.
- Our crew will be at your house to repair the damage within 24 hours.
- We'll make a note on your record and ensure that this doesn't happen again.
- We'll extend our return policy, since this was our mistake.
- We will replace all the … within the next two weeks.
- Our truck will be at your home first thing in the morning.

Offer Solutions

When you can't repair the problem as soon as your customers want, play up the positive side of what you're doing.

When Offering Solutions, Use Words Like These

Only: We will need only a few hours to …

Just: The refund will just take …

First: We will put your order in first thing.

Ahead: Because of our mistake, we will put you ahead of everyone else.

Priority: Resolving this is definitely a priority.

Expedite: We will expedite the shipment time.

Less than: This should take us less than a month.

Here are some other useful solution-oriented phrases:

- Our crew will be at your house as soon as possible—in less than two weeks.
- You will have the refund in only two weeks.
- We will focus on getting this done—it's a priority.
- I will contact the wholesaler first thing in the morning to see what he can do.
- The changes will take only a few weeks—and will be made before Christmas.
- The change will take only three months—usually it takes five.

When Possible, Give a Little Extra

- We're extending the sale date for you.
- Come in and have a meal on the house.
- I'm sending you 10 discount coupons as a way of saying we're sorry.
- We're not going to charge you for service that month.
- We'd like to give you a sample pack of our new …
- I'm not going to charge you for …
- I'll give you a consultation on the phone—no charge.

Show Why the Problem Occurred Whether or Not the Complaint Was Valid

- This occurred because our representative was charging you the old prices; the new ones just came in Friday.
- You have the same name as one of our other customers, and our system confused the two.
- We never received your address change form, and your shipment went to the wrong address.
- Your invoice got lost in the system.
- Our employee was new and credited your account incorrectly.
- This never happened before so we couldn't anticipate it.

Apologize—Be Specific

- I apologize for her behavior.
- I'm sorry about the time involved.
- Sorry about the …
- I apologize for the … Believe me, it will never happen again.

> *Quick tip:* Be careful not to overapologize. You risk making the situation worse than it is, alienating customers even more and possibly setting yourself up for a lawsuit.

Make Future Plans, When Appropriate

- If you want to send other information, please do. Otherwise, I will check in next month.
- Let me know that you received the package.

- I will follow up on your case periodically and let you know if I detect any problems.
- You should hear from our consultant this spring. If you need advice earlier, just call.

End on a Happy Note

- Thanks again for letting me resolve this issue.
- I apologize again—and thanks for being so considerate.
- I appreciate all your patience—you've been a good sport.
- Once again, I apologize and can assure you the situation is completely corrected.
- Thanks for being so understanding. As I said, this won't happen again.

Antsy and Anxious Customers

Antsy customers pace. They fidget. They run their hands through their hair, look around, and generally exude anxiety. And your mission? Especially when there's nothing you can do to help the situation? Give *them* a sense of control so they chill out, relax, and stop irritating other customers. You're probably wondering how *that* is possible. These perfect phrases will show you.

Be Understanding

- Sorry this is taking so long.
- I know this might seem like a long wait.
- I know you've been waiting for …
- I guess this is taking longer than you expected.
- I apologize for the delay.
- This is a longer delay than we predicted.

Explain the Holdup

- We are short one person.
- We got slammed with other orders just before you came in.
- At this time of year, we're always a little slower.
- We are out one machine. While it's being repaired, we only have two, and both of them are working 24/7.
- The weather is bad—too bad we can't control it!
- We just learned the regulations have changed. So now we need to …
- The city now requires that we … so it's taking longer than before.
- We had an emergency, and most of our crew is still at the site.

Show the Benefits of Waiting

Be sure that you're specific when explaining the reason for the wait—otherwise, you risk sounding condescending:

General and condescending: This is for your own good.

Specific: We need to do one more test to make sure your … works correctly.

General and condescending: These things take a long time.

Specific: Because of the … and the … this takes a long time.

Here are a few more phrases:

- We want to test this several times to make sure it's accurate.
- Our first priority is making sure you're safe so we need to …
- It's important that we go through the right channels.
- We need to get the right approvals.

Offer Something to Distract Them

This has the added benefit of helping them feel better about you:

- Would you like a cup of coffee or tea while you wait?
- We have some magazines in the employee lounge. Would you like me to get one for you?
- Please help yourself to coffee and doughnuts.
- I have some information about the product that might help you when you bring it home.

- If you want to wait in the cafeteria, I will come get you when it's your turn.
- We have a vending machine out back. If you want to get something, I'll hold your place.
- Why don't you fill out these forms now? Then when it's your turn, you can be finished that much faster.
- Can I contact anyone for you while you wait?
- If you want to go home or back to work, I can call you when it's ready.
- If you like, I can drive you downtown and then pick you up in an hour or so when it's ready.

Make Them Feel Special

Taking them aside: Just wanted to let you know we're still working on it.

Giving them priority status: I assigned Mr. Rose to your case—he's the best we've got.

Putting them in touch with one of your experts: I'm going to have Rosa, our lead technician, call you about it.

Use Humor, When Appropriate

- I may not be able to stop the thunderstorm, but I can give you a certificate to the airport diner.
- Just be glad our benches are comfortable.
- Well, it sure beats walking through the rain.
- Just think how much you'll appreciate the ... once you get it.
- At least you can get some work done while you wait.
- Not a bad way to spend your time if you're on an expense account—don't you agree?

Help Them Predict

- This shouldn't take too much longer.
- Normally, this only takes an hour, so I assume you won't have to wait too much more.
- You're next in line, so it shouldn't be too long.
- Right now, there are four in front of you.
- If you go online, you'll see how long this will take.
- The average wait is usually …

> *Quick tip:* Update your customers regularly so that they feel greater control and know you haven't forgotten them. Short notes and e-mails work wonders. If the customers are in your waiting room, stop in with an update.

Wrap Up with a Happy Ending

- I appreciate your patience during all this.
- Thanks for waiting.
- Thanks for being a good sport.
- Glad we could get this to you and that everything worked out all right.
- Hope you like this—I think you will.
- So nice to know you finally received it.
- Thanks for waiting and enjoy your day!

How to Help Customers Adapt to Changes

Few people—especially customers—like unexpected change. They *are* paying for the service, after all. And they *are* promised the same process, image, and products cemented in by your brand. So what's an employee to do? Three things: (1) Speak with them directly, person to person and not company to person. (2) Help them see how they benefit from the change. (3) Prepare them for what's ahead so that the first blow is the only blow.

Let Customers Know about the Changes from You First

Broach the Subject on the Phone or in Routine Conversations

- Just wanted you to know we've been bought out by …
- When you look at your bill from now on, it will look different.
- You'll need to call Derry, New Hampshire, now since our office is moving.
- Since you're like one of our family, I wanted to tell you before you read it in the paper.

Be Sure to Place the Good News (for Them) First

- You can still visit us in our Lincoln Center store, but this branch will be closing.
- We have a new Web site, so you will be getting all your information there instead of through this call center.
- The bills will now be more reader friendly, and you can pay online.

- Since we are expanding our product line, we will be moving to a larger building.
- I know you'll enjoy the employees who will be replacing me when I have relocated.
- We're still the same company even though our logo has changed.
- You'll get the same great service from the same employees even though our name has changed.
- You'll get even better products at lower prices now that we've merged.

Use These Phrases in Announcements

- We're happy to announce a new partnership that will bring two leading companies together.
- We want our shareholders to know that in the interests of profit and containing costs, we will be downsizing by 15 percent.
- Customers can now find us in scenic …
- As one of the leading providers of … we're happy to announce …
- We want all our customers to know that as of next Tuesday, …
- We are pleased to let our customers know that …

Use These Phrases in Letters or Memos Attached to Mailers

- Just wanted you to know you should contact Betty as of next week. My position has shifted, and I'll be in accounts payable.

➡

- Just so you know, we're opening a branch in Miami, so I'll be moving there. I've enjoyed knowing you, and I'm sure you'll like my replacement just as much.
- Our CEO has retired, and her replacement is making major changes. As part of the reorganization, I've just been promoted to vice president of major accounts. You can still call me if you need anything though.
- Wanted you to know, this office will be closing next month. You can still find our …
- As you probably know, our company has had to lay off employees. I've decided to take this opportunity to return to school. Please know that I have enjoyed very much having you as a client.

Provide a Q&A Format in Written Documents and Presentations

Make sure the questions sound natural and conversational—whether you give them in a marketing piece, a PowerPoint presentation, or a talk. Here are some examples:

Unnatural question: Please refer to the contact status of all past-due billing under the forthcoming change.

Natural question: Whom should you contact about late bills once you've changed owners?

- I wanted to address some questions that may come up:
  - Why are we closing?
  - What will happen to your account?
  - When will these changes begin happening?
  - Whom should I contact with questions?
  - Do you anticipate a buyout?

Obviously, you must answer each question immediately after you present it. If giving a presentation or holding a meeting, let the participants ask additional questions afterward.

> *Quick tip:* Make sure you standardize the message announcing the change in your memos, phone calls, and meetings with the press. If you're an employee, take the corporate office's lead in positioning the changes.

Show Customers How They Will Benefit

- Now you can visit our three bigger locations.
- This decision is good news for shareholders like you.
- We want to ensure that our customers get superior service, so we are …
- Our focus is on quality, and with these changes …
- We will be able to return to the service you remember from …
- We will be able to expand our offerings, as a result …

Help Customers Predict What to Expect

- You can go on our Web site to learn about changes.
- Over the next few weeks, you can expect …
- The first thing that will happen will be … Then …
- While I'm not sure about details, I do know that …
- According to our CEO, you won't notice much of a difference.
- We'll still be the same company, only under different ownership.

- Because our parent company is larger and more profitable, you can expect positive changes like …
- Most of the changes won't occur for another year.

Reassure Customers

- Our new owners have considerable experience in …
- We had a great talk with the new owners, and I know that …
- Our staff may be moving, but we're not looking for new jobs …
- They are renowned in the field of …
- These changes will definitely make us a stronger company by …
- We've needed these changes for a long time. And the entire staff is happy that they happened.

Use Familiar Language

Avoid heavy bureaucratic language—it sounds unfriendly and cold. Instead, use familiar words that win your customers' trust:

Bureaucratic: In the event that questions should arise, I can be contacted at the above number until July 25.

Familiar: If you have any questions, just call me at … until July 25.

Bureaucratic: Pursuant to our discussion of May 23, from this time forward, all collectibles should be sent to …

Familiar: Send all payments to …

Bureaucratic: This company will decease in its former status as …

Familiar: We will no longer be …

Bureaucratic: The above name will heretofore be changed to …

Familiar: Our company's new name will be …

Use a Comfortable, Possibly Humorous, Tone

- I know you thought you could never live without us, and guess what? You don't have to! We're moving up the street!
- Ever wonder what life would be like with two or three of us? Well, wonder no more—we're expanding.
- Our company just got married. Well, sort of. We were just incorporated into the … family.
- True, we have a new name. And a new look. And even new employees roaming around. But underneath—it's still us.

How to Resolve Billing Problems with Customers

One reason customers get so upset about bills is that they have a built-in mistrust of companies, from small mom-and-pop companies to corporate giants. Well, *especially* corporate giants. Most people believe businesses *will and*— worse—*are* ripping them off, barring a 50 percent off sale. So when billing problems spring up, they launch into defensive mode. As a result, your first step will be to win their trust. *You* rip them off? Mother Teresa is more likely to rip them off. Then go through the objective and indisputable reasons why the situation is the way it is. Was your company to blame? No problem. Were the customers at fault? Let them know ways to avoid the problem in the future.

Use Friendliness from the Start—No Matter How Disagreeable Customers Are Being

- Thanks for bringing this to my attention.
- Let's see how I can help you figure this out.
- Why don't we take a look at your bill and see what's going on.
- My job is to help you.
- We can sort this out.
- I'll be happy to help you. Why don't you tell me what's happening.

Use Calming Language

- I'm sure we can figure this out.
- Don't worry, we'll find a solution.
- If this is the amount you owe, we have plenty of payment options. If not, we'll take care of it right away.

- Don't worry, we'll do what's fair, believe me.
- Let's look at this together.
- Just let me know what you think the problem is, and we'll sort this out.

> *Quick tip:* Speak softly and engage customers as much as possible. They need to feel that they are involved and that the process is transparent.

Refer to the Unambiguous Nature of Bills

- Our billing is regulated by …
- If you look at your policy, you can see exactly how we bill.
- Our ads indicated that the sale was good only for …
- As you can see in your contract …
- The terms and agreements section of your contract states that …
- The contract is a legal agreement, so we need to abide by that. If we billed you the wrong amount, we will definitely correct it.
- We do not determine our prices—they're based on a regulated standard.
- Let's calculate how the billing department arrived at that amount.
- The amount of interest that you pay was established when you signed the contract—it's a legal matter.
- You can get details about our billing policy by going on our Web site … or I can tell you them now.

Avoid Blame

Blaming them: You didn't return our calls.

Being neutral: We didn't hear from anyone even though we left messages with our phone number.

Blaming your company: Our company is really bad at getting bills out.

Being neutral: Things like this happen.

Blaming them: You didn't send the bill in on time.

Being neutral: We didn't receive the bill until October 10—11 days past the due date.

Blaming your company: The bill was filed incorrectly

Being neutral: The numbers in the file were not correct.

Use a Bad News–Good News Approach

Bad news   Good news

(*bad news*) Even though your bill is two weeks late, (*good news*) we haven't sent it to a collection agency yet.

Here are more phrases using this strategy:

- Although we can't accept your checks, we can take a credit card.
- You must pay 10 percent in interest, but we can reduce the total since you're willing to pay in cash.
- Your payment was three weeks late, but if you pay it today, I won't add interest.
- Since you paid an old bill, I won't charge you interest on the delay in your paying the new one.

Send Customers to a Web Site Where You Address Questions

- If you want to learn more about our collections procedures, please go to our Web site at … or call me at …
- You can find a Q&A that will address all your questions on our Web site …
- Please see our Web site to learn more about our policy on late payments.
- Go to our Web site for clear and complete information about our collections policies.
- You can learn more about how to pay electronically—and avoid overdo payments—by going to our Web site at …
- The Web site has a great Q&A that outlines the best way to get your payments in on time and avoid paying interest.

When Customers Are Contesting a Bill, Respond with a Three-Part Approach

1. Consider the Situation—Even If Customers Are Wrong

Do not say: You're wrong about this. You must pay the amount on your bill. Sorry.

Do say: Let's take a look at your bill and see whether it's correct.

Do not say: We couldn't have been wrong. We haven't sent an incorrect bill in the 20 years I've been here.

➡

Do say: Well, we usually don't bill incorrectly; in fact, we haven't been wrong in the 20 years I've been here. But let me look to make sure.

Or use these perfect phrases:

- Why don't you show me exactly what you think the problem is.

- Our billing department is usually on target with bills. But, who knows. Let's look.

- I can see this situation is complex. Let's figure out what's going on.

- If this amount is incorrect, then I definitely want to fix it.

- Let's make sure this is correct. We don't want you to pay more than you should.

2. Review the Facts of the Situation

- I can see that you …

- A few issues may be confusing you: The rates increased in November, and …

- Well, this part looks correct because … Now let's look at …

- What plan are you under?

- When did you purchase this product?

- Do you happen to have your sales slip?

- Let me look up your account on the computer and see what's really going on.

- Let's look at your payment history closely.

3. If Your Company Has Made the Error, Explain to Customers Why They Are Correct

- We accidentally credited your payment to someone with your name.
- Oh—I see what happened.
- Thank you for bringing in your receipts. These helped clarify the situation.
- What happened was …
- Because your billing history is so complex, we accidentally …
- The reason this happened was …
- There are ambiguities in … so we …

Apologize, but don't overapologize:

- Sorry about the mistake.
- Sorry about this problem. I'm happy we could clear it up.
- Thanks for letting me know, and I'm sorry this caused you trouble.
- Accept my apologies. We rarely make mistakes on billing.

Assure them that the problem won't happen again and give the evidence of why:

- Now that … this shouldn't happen again.
- We have changed your information in the system so you should be all set.
- I'll make sure that you are assigned to our veteran financial experts, since your situation is complex.
- The policies rarely change, so this shouldn't come up again.
- Because … happened, you were billed incorrectly. But that's an anomaly, so you should be all set.

➥

- We are going to follow up with your ... to make sure it's all set.

If Customers Have Erred, Tell Them Why They Are Incorrect and Explain the Situation by Using Facts, Not Opinions

- Because you were two weeks late ...
- The interest had accrued ...
- Once we send your account to a collections agency, there's nothing we can do.
- According to your contract, which is a legally binding agreement, ...
- You have a two-week window, but we did not receive the check until ...
- According to our records, we sent you a reminder on ...

Use Positive—and Future-Oriented—Language

Negative: You didn't pay the bill on time.

Positive: You needed to pay the bill on time.

Negative: You didn't sign the agreement form.

Positive: You had to have signed the agreement form.

Negative: You didn't get it in until early November.

Positive: We needed to receive it by September 20, but it arrived in early November.

Negative: We cannot open your account because you haven't paid the back amount.

Positive: We can open your account once you pay the back amount.

Negative: You have a history of waiting until the middle of the month to send your bills.

Positive: Be sure to get your bills out on the first—not in the middle—of the month.

Make Future Plans Whether Customers Are Right or Not

- If you have any questions, call me at this extension.
- Make sure that you fill out the change of address form—that will help a lot.
- If you pay online, we can credit the payment three, even four days faster.
- If you pay on the same day every month, you won't forget to pay the bill.
- Why don't you use the payment form—it will be a lot faster.
- We can e-mail you an acknowledgment, if that will help you feel comfortable.

How to Manage Demanding Customers

Demanding customers are much like demanding children—only you get to leave the customers at the end of the day. Regardless, apply the same principles: Notice them and make them feel special. Give them what they're entitled to, but not too much. Explain in clear, undeniable terms that they can't get what they want—but do give them a concrete reason ... and "Because I said so" doesn't count. Of course, if you *can* satiate their never-ending needs, do so. At once. With enthusiasm. This should make for a better interaction later on.

Give Them Immediate Attention—Even If They Have to Wait

- Nice to see you—I'll be there in one second.
- Just give me a moment, and I'll be right there.
- Give me a moment, would you? I'm rushing, and I'll be right back.
- I just got your message and wanted to get right back to you.
- My assistant just informed me that you called.
- I was just starting off to a meeting, but when I heard you were on the phone, I decided to take the call.
- Please, let me get right back to you. What time works?

If You Don't Connect, Let Them Know How to Reach You

Try to make it special:

- You can call me at ... Or call my cell phone at ... But don't give it out to anyone else.

➡

- I normally leave the office at 2:00. But if you need me later, try my cell phone.
- If I'm not there, ask my assistant to page me.
- If I'm not there, leave the message with my assistant. She'll find me the minute I'm back in the office.
- Leave me a message. If I know it's you, I'll get back right away.
- If you e-mail me, I'll get back to you by the end of the day.
- I'm eager to talk to you—please call me in an hour.
- I can't get out of this meeting—wish I could. Can you call me at 2:00? I'll definitely be free then.
- I can't talk right now, but Charles will help you. He's the best employee we've got.

Or Better Yet, Find Out When They Prefer to Be Contacted

- Let me call you back—what time works for you?
- What day works best for you?
- What is the best way I can reach you?
- Any time that's good for me to call?
- Which do you prefer? E-mail or voice mail?
- I can send someone to your house—just tell me what time.

Apply Focus and Feeling

Focus on them by nodding your head, listening closely, and using these perfect phrases:

- I see …
- Let me get this straight …

- I understand exactly what you're saying …
- Please, give me a few more details so I get a clear picture. For example …
- Interesting …

Acknowledge Their Feelings

- That must be difficult for you.
- I can understand why you have those expectations.
- I can see why you need that so soon.
- Yes, a lot of people feel that way.
- I agree.
- Well, that's understandable.

When You Can Give Them What They Want, Let Them Know—Emphatically

- Yes, I will definitely get it to you by …
- I'm happy to say that we can fill your order at the exact time you want it.
- Yes, I can get you that service. Even better, I can get you …
- For you, I will order both of them. You can expect them as soon as …
- Great news …
- Yes, we absolutely can …
- I'd be more than happy to …
- You know I'm always willing to help in whatever way I can.

Put It in the Positive

Negative: We can't get you the … until March 14.

Positive: We can get you the … before March 15.

Negative: We have only two of these left.

Positive: Great—we have two of these left.

Negative: Your … will need a lot of work.

Positive: We can take care of all the work your … needs.

Negative: We don't have time now.

Positive: I'll make time for you as soon as tomorrow.

Negative: We can't … until tomorrow morning.

Positive: We can … first thing tomorrow morning.

Put the Good News First, and Mention Bad News, Such as Time Delays, Second

- Yes, we can fix your … once we get the part from the distributor. Probably in two weeks.

- We can schedule you for the twentieth if you don't mind paying the extra $20.

- We definitely can get the part for you when you return.

- The job is much easier than we thought. Our expert can get to it on …

- When found both of the … you want. They're in a warehouse in Tibet, but we'll get them as quickly as we can.

- This is the highest quality … available, and it's certified … which is why it costs more.

Cite a Source or Objective Reason Why They Can't Get What They Want

Preface First So That They Feel Important

- Because you're a regular …
- I want to make this work out for you.
- I know this is important to you.
- I tried every possible avenue.
- I looked everywhere, but couldn't find …
- If we have it, you'll be the first one to get it.

Explain the Situation

- We tried everyone, even our online networks, but we can't find it.
- Our agreement prohibits us from doing that.
- According to company policy, we can … only when …
- I would, but the law requires that we …
- This would be possible if …
- If you look on your contract, you'll find that …
- The best we can offer, given your plan, is …

Offer Something Else

- I'm going to put a rush on it.
- I'll assign Juan—he's the fastest.
- I can switch your plan if you like.
- If you decide to get the … instead, I think I can waive the service charge.
- If you get the … instead, I can make sure that you get it by next week.

- Let me put you on our waiting list.
- I'm going to bump you ahead on our waiting list since you're such a loyal customer.
- Because this means so much to you, I'm going to …
- How about if I have our store in San Diego ship one? Normally they won't do this kind of thing, but I think I can convince them.
- We have only two of the other. If you want, I'll reserve those. But you have to let me know right now—they're going quickly.

Part Six

Perfect Phrases for Communicating with Difficult Vendors and Employees from Other Departments

N aturally, you expect visitors to your office to be on their best behavior. After all, they represent their company or department. And at least with vendors, you are the client. You are paying their bills. You are working together for a common goal. Aren't you?

So when these should-be-easygoing workers end up sabotaging your plans, what do you do? Certainly you can't fire them—at least not right away. As everyone knows, skilled contractors can be hard to find. And you can't demote them or write new objectives for next year, since you're not their boss. But you can assert your authority and get clear and specific results by communicating the right message at the right time. Here are some ideas:

- *Keep records.* Most likely, you have records about bills, roles and responsibilities, and project terms. But document every meaningful conversation or decision in a meeting. Make sure that you e-mail the contractor and provide the opportunity to change or clarify any points. This may prove your saving grace if the contractor reneges on the deal or, just as likely, denies it ever existed. By the way, the more specific, the better. "Early delivery" could mean "weeks" to the contractor and "minutes" to you.
- *Think outcomes—not actions.* When negotiating terms, whether for support staff in your office or for a delivery of computer parts, outline the *outcomes* you expect. This will ensure that you don't pay for a consultant who walks in and out the door every day but rather for a consultant who drafts critical information in a report. Oh, and while you're at it, be sure to mention the kind of information you

need, how much of it you need, and how you're going to use it. You don't want to pay for useless details or pay twice for getting what you asked for.

■ *Articulate expectations in your terms.* Did the vendor neglect to send you a shipment on time? Did your contractor miss work three days in a row? It's one thing to complain. It's another to assert your expectations: what you want in the future and how the vendor can make up for the past. Don't leave that decision up to him or her by the way—be precise. Reveal the cost of their actions to you and accept payment for that amount. And yes, you will need to negotiate, but by being clear, you'll control the terms.

Stay tuned: In the following sections, you'll get perfect phrases to help.

How to Control a Coworker from Another Department in a Meeting with Customers

You know how it is—you're in a meeting with a customer, important client, or employee from another department. Naturally, you want to make a good impression—not just for you, of course, but for your fellow employees back in the office, your boss, your entire department, and even your entire corporation. All is going well except for one 200-pound glitch—who happens to be in a suit and tie beside you. I am referring to none other than that coworker who's been assigned to your team from another department. You know, the one who doesn't have the good sense to be humble, respectful, or agreeable. So how do you salvage the talk? Stay calm, be cool, and try for subtlety. These phrases will definitely help.

Apply Damage Control

Provide a Game Plan Before the Meeting

- I know this guy complains a lot, so we have to be low key.
- He works for the CEO, so we have to let him take control of the meeting.
- She's pretty sensitive, so just smile and be polite.
- I've worked with him before—he's loud and argumentative, but he'll go along with our ideas. So let him vent, and we'll the keep the conversation going.
- She is really forgetful, so we need to casually remind her of what we agreed on the last time we were here, okay?
- He keeps interrupting, but don't try to stop him or he'll embarrass you. If you feel like we missed any points, we can always e-mail his boss later.

Determine Roles, and If Your Coworker Is Difficult, Be Discreet

- Why don't you talk about the technology, and I'll cover the rest?
- Let me answer her questions, since I've worked with her countless times before, okay?
- Why don't you introduce the topics, and I'll take it from there.
- I think you're great at explaining how the system works. Let me take over about timing and prices.
- Let me handle this customer. She's tough, and I know what she needs on this project.
- Let me discuss the … You focus on the … since you're an expert.

> *Quick tip:* Try to convince your coworker that you're working as partners—not competitors. Together you'll get great results.

Send Signals

Give the employee a penetrating look, nod, or other nonverbal signal. If that fails, make suggestive comments.

When Your Coworker Interrupts the Customer

- Hold on a second. Let me hear what he's saying.
- Wait one minute. What were you saying [*to the visitor*]?
- One moment. I don't think he was done.
- Just a second. Were you done [*to the visitor*]?

➡

When Your Coworker Starts Arguing a Point

- Let's back step a second…
- Actually, I want to be clear about what Betty's saying.
- Wait a minute. I think Dana is making an excellent point, and I'd like to hear more.
- You're making a good point, but I think we need to hear Joyce right now.

When a Hot Conversation Ensues

Cool your coworker first:

Do not: Be careful not to accuse, reprimand, or overtly contradict the coworker, because those actions will give customers the impression that your company is not cohesive and that you're ultimately not in control.

Do: Lead the conversation to a place of agreement.

Don't accuse: That's completely untrue, and you know that, Paul. This is the best methodology we could use.

Lead: Actually, you may have been right two weeks ago, but now …

Don't accuse: You don't know what you're talking about, Paul. This isn't your area of expertise, so you shouldn't get involved in the first place.

Lead: Actually, you may be confusing this with some of the other tools we explored.

Don't accuse: Don't contradict me, Paul. It's rude, and what you're saying is inaccurate.

➥

Lead: Actually, we tested this system, and it is clearly the best for the data we want.

> *Quick tip:* Let your coworker's manager know about the problem. Be specific about your coworker's exact words, facial expressions, and body language.

How to Silence a Coworker Who's Disagreeing with You in Front of Visitors

- We'll address that issue later.
- I think we discussed this earlier and came up with different conclusions.
- Let's stay on track—we'll discuss that issue later.
- We should discuss … instead.
- Why don't we ask the boss later? It sounds like we're probably both right.

How to End a Disagreement with an Employee in Front of Others

- Let's stick to what we know, for now.
- What you're saying sounds right, but the tests prove otherwise.
- I'm glad you mentioned it, but I think that …
- Thanks for bringing that up because it actually supports what I'm saying. Here's how: …
- Let's look at the facts. Here's what they tell us.
- That point actually suggests an interesting possibility: …

End on a Positive Note

- Thanks for meeting with us—I think this was productive.
- I appreciate your time. You had some great insights, and I know we'll use them.
- This was a really helpful talk. I'll get back with you soon.
- Thanks for sharing your perspectives. They were really helpful.
- I'm definitely going to be thinking about this meeting. It really brought up some interesting and important points.

Record the Event to Protect Yourself in the Future

- During the meeting, Jake used strong language including …
- The customer made three fact-based points … Jake replied by saying …
- Jake told the client that we could not … even though our policy clearly states that we can.
- When I signaled that he should switch the subject, he replied …

Quick tip: Rely on facts including specific words, times, and numbers—do *not* use subjective or emotional words such as *embarrassed me* or *got really rude* or even *insulted the client*. Instead, *show* how this happened.

Send the Customer Corrections If Need Be

- Just wanted to update you about what I've discovered since our discussion

- Just wanted to let you know that I agree with your point about …
- I reviewed the proposal, and you are correct in saying that …
- You were right in your calculations about … Thanks for standing behind your point.
- I'm happy to say that your thoughts about … are, indeed, correct.
- Your insights about … will be helpful moving forward.

Difficult Contractors

You'd think vendors would be easy to work with. Friendly. Accommodating. But difficult vendors abound from construction subcontractors to professional services groups. And communicating with them requires strategy, objectivity, and focus on your part to avoid potentially costly outcomes. The perfect phrases here will guide you to getting optimal outcomes, from keeping otherwise easy vendors on your side to getting difficult ones to quietly say good-bye.

Be Clear, Exact, and Specific in Agreements and Roles and Responsibilities Lists

General: You must complete all reports on time.

Specific: You must complete all reports by the fifteenth of this month and provide the following: …

General: Your employees who work on our projects must be qualified.

Specific: Your employees must have the same qualifications for this role as ours do, as defined in our policy on page …

General: You must complete the project on time, as outlined in your plan.

Specific: We expect the first stage of the project to be completed on … according to the plan that you sent us on …

Here are some more perfect phrases:

- You will produce exactly …
- You will supply … who will be on site in our office … days a week from … to … each day.
- By Friday afternoon at 5:00 each week, the temporary employee will have provided exactly …
- Your representatives will make at least … calls a day between … and … Before leaving, they will forward to us their call list, including responses from their targets.
- This project will entail … number of contractors who will work at your facility and send the documented project sheets on …

Give Contractors Responsibility for Outcomes as Well as for Roles

- As a result of your efforts, we will receive … by October 15 at 5:00.
- Specifically, we will go from … to … by … without requiring additional time.
- Our employees will be able to … once you have completed this project. This should not entail additional work from them or anyone else from your agency.
- You employee will … and … and should receive a rating of at least … from our staff after that point.
- Your employee will serve as a … as listed in our roles and responsibilities manual. By the end of her tenure, she should have provided us with …
- Your team will build … number of … by … All of this must be in compliance with our safety code and pass 100 percent of the safety tests.

Pinpoint Behavior Problems

- The manager of your project has been complaining about our employees in group gatherings. In particular, while gathering at our lunch meeting, I heard her refer to our project manager as …

- Your employee must comply with our dress standard. He currently comes to work in jeans and sandals.

- Since your employee has been working for us, three employees have complained to me about a smell from the direction of his office.

- I have asked your employee for her weekly task record and have not received one yet—although she has worked for us for two months.

- Several of our customers have complained that your employee has made "suggestive," "insulting," and "sexual" comments.

Remind Contractors of Your Workplace Culture

- Our culture is one of openness and sharing—we expect the same from anyone who works here.

- We believe in treating everyone—customers, employees, and outside support—with respect.

- Our employees believe in a team approach to all their projects.

- We emphasize collaboration; we can achieve this only if your employees provide the required data regularly.

- We are goal oriented.

- We value honesty and openness, above all.

➡

> *Quick tip:* When citing third-person comments, be sure to quote precisely what the person said. Do not make that accusation yourself—let accusers speak for themselves.

Pinpoint Performance Issues

- She has not provided the manual that we agreed would be forthcoming by November 10.
- Although you were supposed to complete the entryway by August 4, the foundation has not even been laid.
- You were supposed to … by … yet the first stage of … has not been completed yet.
- Your employee was supposed to fulfill these seven tasks, as stated in our agreement. At this point, she has only … and …
- As we stated in our agreement, he must be trained in … Yet he claims he "doesn't know the first thing about it."

Get Specific Agreement on Remedies

- I expect you to tell me exactly how you will remedy the problem and by what date.
- What sort of training do you intend to provide for your employees?
- Since they are two months late, you need to inform us of how you are going to make up for the lost time.
- So we can meet our goals, you must tell us …
- How will you ensure she sends us the data on time, every week, as outlined in our agreement?

➡

Perfect Phrases for Applying Pressure

Show unfortunate outcomes:

- As a result of this error, …
- The delays to this project because of this matter have cost us … in dollars and … in employee time.
- According to our customer, they are no longer engaging our service because your employee …
- Because your employee … we did not get …
- Among other matters, our employees have complained that …
- Among other matters, our clients have complained that …

Come to Understandings about Problems—Be Specific about Results

- I hope you understand the situation. Please contact me with questions. Otherwise, I expect to hear from you about solutions by early next week.
- If you would like to add anything to these comments, please let me know. Otherwise, I expect that we will move forward as you outlined in your revised plans.
- As we agreed, to address this problem you will …
- Unless you have any changes, I will consider this plan a commitment as we move forward.

- As you stated, you will replace them with two employees who have the required credentials.

Use a Two-Three-Four Approach

- We already asked you to ... in our May 4 e-mail ... When will you have this done?
- This is the third time I have asked you for this ... I will not ask again.
- This is the second time that we reminded you of ... What will you do to get this done?
- We contacted you twice by e-mail and once by phone about this matter, yet you haven't responded.

Quick tip: Yes, threaten legal action, but only if you plan to follow through.

Difficult Vendors and Suppliers

You'd expect vendors and suppliers to break their necks trying to please you. You know, be polite, send the right products, and beg for mercy when they're one item off. That's what you do for your customers, right? But reasoning is a black hole with some vendors: Ask for 18 of something and they send you 5 … and expect *you* to apologize.

To keep them in line or to get them in line in the first place, you must be clear about your expectations, especially when they drop the metaphorical (and sometimes literal) ball. Remember, you are the customer. And if they want to keep you, they had better behave. And trust me, with these perfect phrases, they will.

How to Handle a Vendor Who Is Late on a Shipment

Be Clear about When You Should Have Received the Shipment

- You agreed to get us the delivery by March 4.
- In our phone conversation, you agreed to get us the delivery two weeks early—on April 16. I e-mailed you a confirmation the day we had the discussion.
- According to your contract, we should receive all shipments within two weeks after the order. I had to wait one month, as you can see on my original order form and the receipt the day I received it.
- Your e-mail stated that you could get me the order by Wednesday.
- Your ad says that you guarantee all shipments in two weeks.

➡

- When my purchasing representative called, you confirmed that we would have the order by Friday.

Let the Vendor Know When You Actually Received It

- It's Monday and we just received it.
- We didn't receive it until the twenty-fifth.
- You delivered only half the order at that time—which was never part of the agreement.
- We received it the following morning when no one was here to move it.

How to Handle a Vendor Who Is Early on a Shipment

- We have no warehouse space for this product.
- The shipment is three days early, and we have nowhere to put it. If you want to find us storage space and pay for it, fine. But we don't have the room.
- You agreed to get us the shipment on Monday morning, not Friday afternoon. It will spoil over the weekend.
- Please review our order form. For three years, we have always received our shipments on …

Quick tip: The more precise you are in stating the time and date you should have received the order, the more room you'll have for negotiating later.

How to Handle a Vendor Who Sends You the Wrong Product

- We needed … of size … so we could assemble our …
- I already have the … in stock. What I need is …

- Our advertisement specifically said we carry … because that's what we ordered. But you sent …
- I cannot use this order at all because …
- Although this is a new model, it isn't the right one. What I ordered was …
- The order form specifically states that I wanted … but I received …

Regardless of Whether the Vendor Is Early or Late or Has Sent the Wrong Order, Explain the Repercussions

- We missed the Christmas rush on those products. Now we probably won't move them for months, and they'll take up valuable shelf space.
- It cost us … in profits what we normally make on that product.
- Many of our customers had to go elsewhere because we didn't have that product—and they bought other products there too. I cannot imagine the cost.
- We were unable to complete the … for our customer on time.
- We had to purchase the order, at greater expense, from a retail store so we could get our client the … on time.
- Our advertising said that we were having a 10 percent off sale on products including that shipment of … As a result, we must …
- Legally, we have to … which means we must …
- Our customers have called demanding … and we need to …

➡

- Our employees were unable to … As a result, we …
- We promised our customer at least …

How to Negotiate a Deal with a Vendor

Remind the vendor of your value as a customer:

- We have been a regular customer for almost 15 years.
- As you know, we order from you all year, which is good news for your cash flow.
- We are willing to pay on the spot.
- For 10 years, we have been a good, steady customer.
- Our outlets order more of the … than any other in this region.
- We have purchased more of your product than any other large store, including …
- We have always had a very easy, friendly relationship, and I would like it to stay that way.
- We have sent many customers your way over the years, including …

> *Quick tip:* If a new owner took over for the old one, be sure to remind the owner of your history, your expectations of prompt deliveries, and the possibility that you will go elsewhere if the service doesn't change.

When Negotiating a Deal, Take a Two-Part Approach

1. State What You Want

- We are entitled to a have a discount on the next delivery.
- I don't want to pay delivery fees on the next order.

- I do not want to pay for the storage fee.
- I want you to take back the order and send me a fresh supply at the appropriate time. I can't use these, and they'll only spoil.
- If you can't take it back, I don't want you to charge me for it.
- If I take it, I want to pay only half.
- I'd be happy with …
- I'd be willing to forget the whole thing for …
- If you are willing to … I won't mention this again.

2. Get the Vendor to Agree

- Do you agree?
- Does that seem fair to you?
- I think that's right, don't you?
- That's a common approach, don't you agree?
- This is a standard solution, right?
- Doesn't this seem right to you?
- That should make up the difference, don't you think?
- A discount of 25 percent seems like a good amount. What do you think?
- I want to know what you think is fair.
- That sounds okay, but I'd be more comfortable with a full 20 percent.
- Don't you agree another delivery makes sense?
- That's fair, wouldn't you say?

How to Handle a Rude Vendor

Whether it's to you or your employee, review and demand is a great approach:

Review   Demand

(*review*) You said that … (*demand*) If you don't fulfill that commitment, I'll have to find another supplier.

Here are a few more examples:

- You refused to move those boxes from the doorway, and as a result, our customers couldn't get through. If you can't be inconspicuous, you'll need to use the back door even though it is much harder to reach from the parking lot.
- You swore in front of my customers. Please don't do that again.
- You pushed one of my customers aside so that I could sign the order. In the future, please wait to the side until I have finished my transaction with my customer.
- You left the order in the main office, and my employees had to spend half an hour moving it. Next time, bring the order directly to the supply room.

How to Speak to the Vendor's Manager

- Your employee refused to stack the boxes in the corner, and our customers had to step around them. Next time, please make sure he's more accommodating or send me someone who is.
- When I asked your employee to put the order in our supply room, she said … In our organization, we treat everyone civilly. We expect the same from our vendors.

➡

- I overheard your employee say " ... " I want a formal apology from your company and a new delivery person.

How to Handle Third-Party Situations

If you're relying on third-party information, do not accuse. Instead, state that someone else has made an accusation and then quote that person directly:

- According to my customer, your employee called her a " ... "
- According to my purchasing representative, your employee said that " ... " I would like you or your employee to address this situation.
- My employee said your representative called him a " ... " I want him to receive a formal apology.

How to Negotiate Finances with Difficult Vendors and Contractors

Money can be a difficult topic to discuss. In fact, it's taboo in many social settings. So when you're discussing rates or prices with a difficult vendor, the subject can be especially sticky. The best way to keep you, and the arrangement, misery free is to be as clear and concrete as possible. No price is ever too high, but it can be 20 percent higher than other people charge. No number is too small, but it can be 20 pieces fewer than you agreed on. And rely on previous agreements, whether written or spoken, whenever you negotiate. Stuck? Not sure what to say? The following perfect phrases will certainly help.

When the Price Goes Up Unexpectedly

- You did not indicate that you were increasing your price, so your bill is 15 percent higher than I expected.
- When you bid for the project, your fee was … Now you are billing at … which is … higher than you committed to charge us.
- We agreed to pay a set amount of … When we received your bill, it was for … higher than that amount.
- When we agree to the hourly fee, it was for the life of this project. However, you wrote in your invoice that you raised your fee by 15 percent to allow for a rise in the cost of living expenses. We never agreed to that amount.
- We negotiated a price of … which is 10 percent less than the normal fee because of volume. Yet your bill does not reflect that agreement.
- Originally, you charged us … Yet your price has gone up without our knowledge.

➡

When Requesting Money Off for a Partial or Damaged Shipment

State what you expected, what you got, and what you want:

- We ordered a shipment of 100 pieces. Yet we found that 26 of these were damaged, and we will need to send these back. As a result, I want you to pay for the shipping costs and replace the 26 pieces at a discount.
- We expected to receive a shipment of … But we received only … Therefore, we want the remaining parts delivered to our office for no additional fee.
- On our order form, we requested … of paper, but we received only half the amount. We had to purchase the difference at full price from a retail store to keep up with our work flow. When you send the remaining order, I think it's fair that we receive a discount.
- Several pieces of our order were unusable because … Please replace those items at no additional cost or delivery fee. We will send the damaged items back COD.

When Requesting Money Off for a Problem Contractor

- We agreed that your employee would … and … Yet she has arrived at work two hours late every day, as you can see from the enclosed documentation, and she has completed only … I would like this to be reflected in your bill.
- Your employee stated that she needed to work from home for personal reasons but would complete the … and … which would be possible in the allotted time. Yet she completed none of these tasks, as you can see from the attached e-mail. Please reflect this in your billing.

- We agreed to pay a monthly fee, assuming that your employee would work eight hours a day, five days a week. However, she has missed three days this month, as we have documented. Please reflect these absences on your bill.

When the Vendor Didn't Provide the Service It Billed You For

- You agreed to … for a price of … But you only … Please adjust the bill accordingly.
- In our agreement, on page 32 you stated that you would supply three full-time employees to our office. Yet between December 1 and January 5, only two of them appeared regularly. Please confirm the attached time sheets and adjust your bill according.
- In our contract, in paragraphs 3 and 4 you stated that your employees would create … by … We have not received the … , yet you have billed us for it.
- Your proposal states that you will provide … for … Yet you gave us only … Therefore, we should pay…
- Our statement of work called for an employee with an undergraduate degree or higher in graphic design. Your employee told us her degree is in fine arts and she has no graphic design experience whatsoever. As a result, we have had to subcontract the task, on short notice, to a freelance designer at an additional expense. We assume your bill for next month will reflect this additional expense on our part.
- Your statement of work said you would fulfill these tasks to completion … Yet you only … Therefore, we would like you to reduce your bill by…

When the Vendor Didn't Credit You for a Payment

- We paid you for the service on July 29 by credit card. Our records show that the payment went through three days later. Please ask your representative to stop contacting us about this matter and check and adjust her records accordingly.

- We paid the … bill on … The check cleared on … Yet on … and … , we have received calls insisting that we pay the full amount. Please adjust your records and stop calling us.

- We received a bill on … We paid it one week later on … At that point, the payment was not late—and would not be for another two weeks. Yet in your … e-mail, you insisted that we pay a late fee.

- We paid you for the order in two installments a week apart. The second installment was a day late. We do not feel we should pay the full late fee as the late payment represented only a part of the total payment.

Quick tip: Send or direct the vendor to materials that will support your case. This will save the time and misery involved in back-and-forth conversations and protect you should legal issues ensue.

Disruptive Participants in Presentations

Anyone who's given a presentation knows the sting of having disruptive employees in the audience. They have different reasons for their responses, and like most workplace issues, it's important not to take them personally. The tricky part, of course, is that the dynamic with groups is entirely different from one-on-one meetings. You can't very well stop the whole presentation to get to the root of the problem. Or whip out an agreement about job responsibilities and so on to make sure the disruptive employee stays on track. Instead, you need to balance the energy in the room so that everyone stays focused while addressing the wild card who sits in the corner.

Participants can disrupt your presentation in countless ways—and each one requires a different solution. We'll look at the classics—with phrases that squelch each one. But first, the basics.

Write an Agenda

- We are going to cover these three points in 15-minute increments. If you don't get your points in at that time, you can follow up with e-mails to me.
- We have only one hour to discuss these points. So I'm going to ask you to limit your comments so everyone can contribute to the discussion.
- I want to cover these four issues … so that we can determine …
- Our goal is to create …
- Here's what we're going to accomplish today: …

> *Quick tip:* Watch for body language—in this case, yours. Are you expressing fear? Anger? How are you using the props around you? Are you sitting at the head of the table, giving the impression of power? Or are you sitting across the table, giving the impression of equality? Are you meeting in a conference room, which is neutral space, or your office? These details can affect how an employee perceives and retains your message.

Call Participants by Name

- As Kathryn said a few minutes ago …
- Let's discuss Luke's concern again. It does raise some interesting points.
- Peter, what do you think?
- I remember that this group thought … ; isn't that correct, Julie?
- I'd like you to give us some input, Sam.
- What is your name? Eric? Thank you. What do you think, Eric?
- What would you do in that situation … Excuse me, what is your name? Sandra? What would you do, Sandra?
- Good insight, Marcus.
- Excellent point, Larry. Do you have anything to add, Nina?

Talk a Little about Your Background—in the Context of Your Point

- I came in from New York today.
- This reminds me of what one of my kids would say: …

➡

- When I was in college in …
- I'm from the Midwest, so I see everything as …
- As they say in New York City where I'm from, …

Now here are some pointers for addressing the classic types of disrupters.

How to Handle Angry Participants

When Addressing a Good Point from an Angry or Outspoken Participant

- Thank you for bringing that up. I'm going to address that point in a few minutes.
- That's an interesting point. Here's what you should consider …
- Thank you for raising that concern. We'll return to it throughout this discussion.
- That's a good point—and others have raised it. Here's what current thinking tells us.
- I'm glad you raised that point—many people have mentioned it before.

When Addressing a Bad Point from an Angry Participant

- Yes, many people feel that way. The truth is that …
- Thank you for bringing that point up. It's a common misconception, and I'd like to address it.
- That's an interesting point, but the facts don't support it. For example, …
- If you look at the studies though, you find that isn't what occurs. For example, …

➡

When Addressing Objections

- How do you think we can avoid those problems?
- Let me write these objections down. Why don't you come prepared to discuss solutions next week?
- What do you think we should do then?
- What are some alternatives that could get us the same results?
- Actually studies indicate that that won't occur.
- Our experience shows that's not the case. Here are two examples.
- That might be true, but if so, let's look at other possibilities.

When Diffusing Anger

- Let's write those thoughts on the flip chart. Then let's write a list of corresponding suggestions about how to deal with them.
- Let's talk about that at the break. For now, we need to stay focused.
- This is an interesting concern. Would anyone like to address it?
- Lots of people in other organizations feel this way. Here is what they've done.

How to Handle Meetings When Several People Are Being Disruptive

- It's critical that we focus on getting an outcome from this meeting. So I expect that everyone will listen when someone is speaking and wait until breaks to leave the room.

- We are a professional organization, and I want everyone to act that way, in this and every other meeting. If you want to know more precisely what I mean by certain statements I am making, please schedule a meeting in my office.
- I notice that some of you are commenting on other people in this room. This must stop immediately because such comments are unprofessional.
- If you have a comment, please address it to everyone in the room, and wait until it is your turn to speak.
- Since we have a strong agenda, we need to focus closely. If you have additional thoughts or comments, please make an appointment to see me later or e-mail me your concerns.

How to Handle Unresponsive Participants

The best way to deal with unresponsive groups is to get them actively engaged. You can do this by asking questions. Use any of the five "W's"—who, what, when, where, and why—and of course, how. Here are a few examples:

- What would you do in that situation?
- What kind of problems do you think this model will help you resolve?
- Where do you think the problem lies?
- Who do you think was correct in this example?
- When would you take steps to resolve this problem?
- When have you experienced similar situations at work?
- Why do you think situations like these occur?
- Why would you use this concept at work?

- How can you apply this concept to your work?
- How many times a day do you think you encounter this?

Of Course, You Can Always Rely on Other Questions as Well

- Can anyone give me an example of a problem you could solve using this system?
- Should this matter be considered important? Why or why not?
- Could you have found a better solution?
- Under what circumstances would you apply this formula?
- Would you approach this differently, and if so, why?

Don't Get a Response?

Address one person in the room who will probably answer because he or she is on the spot, and others may open up as a result. Remember to keep the tone open and friendly:

- Why don't you tell me about a few situations particular to your workplace, Julie?
- I'd like this fellow in the front row to look for any peculiarities in this outline. Don't worry about making a mistake. You can't be wrong here.
- Just for the fun of it, I'd like to ask you, as the department manager, …
- So clue us into your thoughts, Mr. Riley.
- Any thoughts you'd like to share, Ms. Harrelson? I'm really interested in what you think.

> *Quick tip:* Give them an exercise that will create interaction. Say you're using a case study in the presentation. Divide the participants into groups and have them present alternatives or likely outcomes. Or have individuals write down three ideas and ask them to read each aloud.

Be Sure to Create a Framework When Provoking Interaction

- Write down at least three solutions that would help solve the problem.
- Go from the most to the least important.
- What are the top five?
- What is the most obvious … ? Now what are the least obvious? You may need to search here.
- Moving from the left to the right, what do you think are …
- How many …
- Of all the possibilities, write down the most likely to occur … Good, now write down the least likely.

Have the participants read their solutions, and you, and others in the group, can comment on them.

How to Handle In-and-Out Participants

These participants dart in and out of the room. Sure, it's tempting to ignore these interruptions, but don't. You must keep the group focused. Besides, when participants are coming and going, they are sending a clear "other things are more important" message. Here are some perfect phrases to help.

Announce a Break

First, announce that you'll be taking a break or ending the presentation shortly when the disruptive participant person starts to leave the room:

- We'll be taking a break in …
- As I announced at the beginning of the talk, we'll take a break every hour on the hour.
- We're breaking in about …
- We're going to finish up in …
- This session will end in about …
- We have only … left in this session.
- We'll be done in …
- We have a lot to cover in the remaining …

Ask Them to Stay

Then request that everyone stay seated unless there's an emergency so that you can cover everything on the agenda without interruption:

- Please remain seated until the break.
- So that everyone can participate without interruption, please stay seated until the break.
- Unless it's an emergency, please remain seated until 12:15.
- We'll break at 1:00. Until then, please stay in the room.
- So that you don't disturb everyone else, please leave at the break.
- We need to work in break-out groups, so it's critical that you remain in the room until the break.
- If you've finished your exercise, please remain seated, as we'll begin again shortly.

➡

If All Else Fails, Speak to Them Directly

- It's really important that you remain seated during this presentation.
- If you need to come and go, I can let you know when we'll be breaking so that you can plan around that.
- If you need to leave for a specific purpose, let me know, and I can modify the break schedule, if possible.
- Could you please stay until the break?
- If you need to come and go, it's probably better if you don't attend the session, although I'd like to have you. You're missing too much content and disrupting everyone else's focus.

Quick tip: Nonverbal communication is often optimum. Each time employees get up to leave the room, stop talking. Wait until they have left the room to begin again. When they return—same thing. The uncomfortable silence as they walk to and from their seats will keep them from too many exits. If the group is hostile or unusually difficult, save the discussion until the break.

How to Quiet an Outspoken Employee

- Thanks, we'll get to that point later.
- Good point—I'll write it down and we'll return to it later.
- Thanks for that perspective. For now though, hold off and we'll get your perspective later.

- I appreciate those points. Now I'd like to hear from others in the group.
- All those points are really interesting, but we need to move on or we'll never make our goals for this meeting.

How to Keep the Subject on Track

- We need to stick to the agenda. If you have other points, let's see if we can fit them into another meeting.
- If we're going to meet our goals, we need to stay on track.
- You may want to discuss those points after the meeting and e-mail your thoughts to the rest of us.
- We only have 15 minutes left. I'd like to discuss those points further, but we don't have enough time.
- Unfortunately, we have a lot to cover and not a lot of time.
- That's great, but we need to focus on other topics for this meeting.

> *Quick tip:* Slide shows such as those used with PowerPoint, although they are standard in most presentations, rarely help employees grasp and retain your message, particularly when emotionally charged. The word use is usually stilted, the meaning compacted in every slide, and the visuals are usually a distraction rather than a support. So if you must, use slides sparingly. Instead, keep a white board or flip chart nearby so you can address concerns as they come up.

Epilogue: Perfect Phrases for When That Difficult Employee Is You

So, we've talked about difficult coworkers, impossible bosses, unfriendly vendors, and ridiculous customers. But what happens if that difficult person is you? Don't think it's likely? If you see this book in the hands of someone in the next cubicle and that person is flipping to the section on perfect phrases for difficult coworkers, that could be a clue.

Of course, be on the lookout for other clues as well. You may be thinking of obvious ones, such as whether or not you were invited to the last office party. Or those insulting words your boss wrote in your evaluation. Or, even worse, the fact that you didn't get that raise you so richly deserved. Useful—yes. But beware. Take that office party—maybe you were out the week your coworkers held it. And the evaluation? Your boss may be like those restaurant critics who never give more than two stars. As for the raise? Profits are down, and everyone knows it.

On the other hand . . . there's an old saying: "If a hundred Frenchmen tell you you're drunk, you had better sit down." And the clues may point directly to reality. If so, don't worry! The best thing you can do is identify the problem, make changes, and move on to bigger and better steps in your career

Epilogue

The real indicators, though, may be the silent ones—those that accumulate in your head, circle around, and reappear moments later. Do you think negative thoughts about, say, 90 percent of the people in your office? Are you incredulous about how unqualified your boss (and her boss) is for the job?

Of course, those thoughts don't have to occur only at work. Maybe you mutter to yourself about how much you hate the job...before you've even stepped out of bed and had that first cup of coffee. Or perhaps you peruse the employment section of the newspaper and think those entry level jobs have *got* to be better than yours...if only you didn't need the money. Either way, take the hint. You're probably no treat to work with, which is bad news for everyone—especially you.

Then again, you may be impossible...but only in certain circumstances or when working on certain projects. Or maybe the problem really *isn't* you—the job really *does* stink, and your boss really *is* miserable, and your coworkers really *are*, objectively speaking, dolts. Regardless, your mission is to find out. And these perfect phrases, which you can use inside your head...and out...will definitely help.

Is the Problem You? Deciding from the Inside . . . Out

Ask Yourself These Questions to Determine Whether the Problem Is a "Them" or a "You"

- How much time do I spend thinking negative thoughts?
- Do other people agree that . . . is a problem, or are they just being polite?
- Have I experienced this problem in other jobs? With other people?
- Do I respond to people on time?
- When we have team meetings, do I actually listen to other points of view?
- How well do I contribute to my team? Am I able to be both a leader and a follower as events require?

When Possible, Get Specific to Gain Insight into Your Own Behavior

- Claire is chatty. Is that the problem, or is her work style really inept?
- At what point in my last few jobs did I get this dissatisfied? Am I falling into a pattern?

Need an Attitude Adjustment? These Perfect Phrases Should Help

Don't Say

- I'm such an idiot. I had better cut this out!
- I can't help the people on my team if I don't like them. I never like them. Maybe I should just ignore them.
- This is crazy? Why am I doing this?

➡

- I had better watch out, or I'm going to blow any chances for a promotion.
- If I blow it, my family will hate me.

Do Say
- How can I change this pattern?
- What are some ways I can learn to get along with these people?
- What are five good things about this job?
- Claire is a lot like my mother-in-law. What strategies do I use to get along with her?
- I know I won't blow it—I have lots of successes in my life, and this can be one more.